Bitter Truth: My Story of Bitterness, Grace, and Repentance
Study Guide - 10 Lessons in Bitterness
Copyright © 2018 by Linda R. Graf
Published by Cross to Crown Ministries, Colorado Springs, CO 80919
www.crosstocrown.org

ISBN: 978-0-9987863-1-5

Cover by Daniel Davidson, Dan Design LLC, Colorado Springs, CO
bydan.us

Printed in the United States of America.

Table of Contents

Introduction: Guarding Ourselves Against Sin

Welcome! This study guide is intended to accompany the book, *Bitter Truth: My Story of Bitterness, Grace and Repentance* by Linda R. Graf. I (Linda) wrote the book after God did extensive work in my heart and convicted me of bitterness. Although I was a Christian, I had lost all joy in my Christian walk and found myself angry at everyone, almost constantly. I was also consumed with self-pity over the hard things that had occurred in my life. I was fixated on my problems and drowning in sadness, hurt, and anger. The worst part was that I didn't know what was wrong or how to fix it. The Lord was abundantly gracious and merciful to me during this time and led me to His wisdom and godly counsel. It was a long and difficult process, but on the other side of it all, I found renewed hope and joy in Christ. This is what I want for you, too!

But… you may ask, "What if I'm not bitter? Why should I read this book or do the study?"

My Reply: I sincerely hope you're *not* bitter. I pray that you are not because it will save you much grief and heartache. But… you've certainly been angry, right? No one can say they are never angry. And maybe you are angry at the same things or people fairly often. If that's true, you may be in danger of being tempted toward bitterness. You may not have joy and a meaningful, fulfilling walk with Jesus if you are consumed with regular frustration or resentment.

In John 10:10, Jesus said that He came to bring us abundant life, life to the fullest. This is the way it's supposed to look for us as believers and is what makes our faith attractive to a lost world. An abundant life is one with purpose and hope. In contrast, we're told that our enemy desires to kill, steal, and destroy our faith, our hope, and even our very lives. We must seek to uproot anything that gets in the way of living the life Jesus calls us to. We must not be naïve or ignorant of the ways the enemy will try to thwart us.

Why Should You Do This Study?

Reason 1: We must always be on guard against sin in our lives and understand how and where the enemy tries to get in and tempt us.

Scripture has much to say about anger, temptation, and sin, and how to fight it. We learn about the weapons at our disposal as God's beloved children. Studying God's Word also helps us better understand how to live as followers of Jesus and the ways the Spirit of God helps us in the journey.

1. Review and list the weapons we have at our disposal in the armor of God listed in Ephesians 6:11-18. Which are for offense and which are for defense?

Reason 2: There may be someone in your circle of influence who struggles with anger or bitterness. Having a clear grasp of what it is may help you understand and encourage them to repentance and godliness.

2. According to Hebrews 3:12-13, what should be our role in helping our brothers and sisters?

Reason 3: All study of Scripture is a worthwhile endeavor. We will be better able to discern truth from lies and know God's will the more we know God's Word.

3. Read 2 Timothy 3:16-17. How does Paul say that Scripture will profit us?

So, dear friend, whether you are personally tempted to bitterness or not, a study of God's Word is never a fruitless exercise.

Read Chapters 3 and 4 (pp. 21-35) in *Bitter Truth*. They describe my childhood and some challenging situations I faced.

4. Are there any similarities in your upbringing?

5. What are some events in my story that you believe may have contributed to my bitterness?

6. Why couldn't I forgive Phil? (p. 33)

7. What painful events in your childhood stand out to you?

8. What were your responses to these events?

9. How did your family handle conflict?

10. Do you believe there are bitter people in your extended family? How do they influence you or what is your reaction to them?

Dear Lord, may You work in our hearts; convict if necessary and teach us what You'd have us to learn. Help us to live in the abundant life You promise us. May the Holy Spirit illuminate our hearts and minds as we dive into this study.

Lesson 1: Exploring and Defining Anger

It all starts with anger. Anger is a God-given emotion that was intended for good purposes. But, as with other God-given gifts intended for good, once sin was introduced to the world, we distorted and misused it.

Ponder some of God's other good gifts that we have ruined due to sin:
food, work, sex, and rest.

We all experience anger from time to time. But, anger does not always equal sin.

1. What does Ephesians 4:26-27 say?

2. What is the warning given here?

3. What exactly is a foothold? Use the dictionary, if necessary.

According to author and counselor David Powlison, in his book, *Good and Angry: Redeeming Anger, Irritation, Complaining, and Bitterness,* the definition of anger is simple:

I'm against that + I care about it = Anger

Being against the action and caring deeply about it are both required in order for anger to erupt. If you don't care strongly about the issue, you may be mildly bothered but will not feel anger. Also, if it's not something you have a conviction about, but consider just a matter of taste or opinion, you won't be upset.

For instance, the standard of dress or behavior for one culture may be offensive to others. A woman wearing shorts on a hot summer day would go unnoticed in any American city. However, the same attire in most Muslim countries would be completely unacceptable. Conversely, the restrictions on women in those countries would be considered shocking and unfair to modern American females.

What matters *to you* is what causes you to feel angry. Some people are prone to anger while driving—what we call *road rage*—because they believe strongly that people ought to drive the speed limit and follow all the traffic rules. However, someone like me, who is usually deep in thought while driving and not all that concerned with what other people are doing, isn't bothered. I may be the cause of *another's* road rage, but I don't usually suffer from it. But there are other things that really get to me that may not bother you at all.

4. What are some relatively minor things that cause you to feel irritated or angry?

When anger is righteous, its end goal is restoration. Good anger fixes things, puts them back to the way they should be. We should feel righteous anger over injustice, abuse, and violations against the law and character of God.

Three Criteria of Righteous Anger

- It reacts to a violation against God's laws and character.
- It focuses on God and His kingdom, His rights and concerns. It asks the question, "How are they offending God?" It cares for those who are victimized or oppressed.
- It is accompanied by other godly qualities and expresses itself in godly ways. It seeks to help, to restore things back to the way they should be.

Righteous anger confronts evil in a godly way and calls for repentance and restoration.

Jesus Becomes Angry

5. Read these accounts in the Bible where Jesus is angry and identify how those involved were offending God. What or whom was Jesus angry at?

Mark 3:4-5:

Mark 10:14:

Mark 11:15-17:

John 2:13-16:

However, most of the time, we distort righteous anger and turn it into sinful anger. How do we do that? We make it all about *us*. Our anger is usually about something that personally bothers or upsets us.

Sinful Anger

- Reacts to a wrong or perceived wrong against me.
- Is a reaction to something that offends or bothers me. It focuses on my rights and concerns; how I was inconvenienced, slighted, harmed. I ask the question, "How are they offending me?"

- Is accompanied by sinful and selfish qualities. I accuse, yell, withdraw, or use sarcasm to hurt. I am moved to sinful actions such as revenge or violence. The ultimate goal of my anger is getting my own way.

Sometimes we start out with righteous anger over an injustice or abuse and then react to it in selfish or sinful ways. One good example is disobedient children.

When children are not obeying us, they are sinning; going against the law of God. Furthermore, they may be acting in ways that lead to their ultimate harm. As parents, we are concerned for their safety, maturity and growth. We are responsible for them. It's our duty to correct and punish them when necessary. Our end goal is their repentance and better behavior in the future. This all falls within the scope of righteous anger.

But as a parent, I can tell you that most of the time when I reacted to a disobedient child, I was reacting in sinful and selfish anger. I was frustrated with them for their repeated failure to listen and comply with my commands. I was inconvenienced because they wouldn't do as I desired. I was angry because their failure impacted me and my schedule. If my child was acting out publicly, I was embarrassed by their behavior.

This kind of anger provoked me to yelling, blaming, and speaking unkindly. The fruit of my anger was not Christlike, and *I sinned in response to their sin*. Just because they are in sin doesn't justify my sinful reaction. It's shocking to realize that as parents we are often as much in need of repentance as the disobedient children are.

6. What are some other examples you can think of where righteous anger can turn into sinful anger?

Another component of sinful anger is that we may become angry over a *perceived* offense. The wrong done is only in our imagination. This may happen when we think someone has gossiped about us, resulting in a poor reputation or a missed opportunity. We may guess that someone has spread negative tales about us without even knowing it to be true. Or we may *decide* what someone's intentions toward us are, and be offended by them, even with no concrete evidence.

Other Major Contributors To Sinful Anger

A. Our Unmet Expectations
B. Hurt Feelings

What are expectations? They are the things that *should* happen, according to our view of the world. Expectations also set us up for disappointment and ultimately anger when we don't see things unfold as we believe they ought to.

Read pp. 57-63 in *Bitter Truth*.

7. What is ultimately at the root of expectations?

8. Look up and summarize Proverbs 11:2 and Proverbs 13:10.

9. Can you think of some instances where your expectations often go unfulfilled?

10. How do you react in those situations?

Read pp. 129-136 in *Bitter Truth* on hurt feelings.

11. From the list on p. 130, which ways you are most susceptible to hurt? (Or list your own.)

12. Where does hurt come from?

13. Can we always help feeling hurt?

14. What is the opposite attitude from feeling hurt?

15. Read Philippians 2:3-8 and summarize Christ's humility.

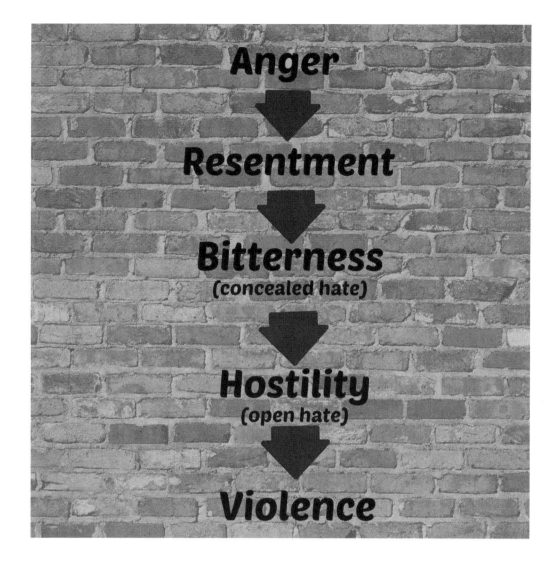

Sinful anger is the doorway to bitterness, hostility, and violence.

The frightening thing about indulging in sinful anger is that it begins a process. Once sinful anger is regularly indulged in, it starts a chain reaction. Anger can grow to eventually become outright violence and even murder.

Author Jerry Bridges defines the process in his book, *Respectable Sins*. Read his comments on p. 48 in *Bitter Truth*.

Sinful anger first grows into resentment. *Resent* comes from an old French word that means "to feel." Once we move into resentment, we are re-living the offense. We are feeling hurt or pain. We remember how unfair it is and rehearse it often.

16. What can happen in cases of resentment? (p. 48)

17. The next step after resentment is full-fledged bitterness. Read the definition on pp. 48-50 and list some characteristics of a bitter person.

18. Think back to your childhood. Were there events that caused you to be angry or resentful? How do you feel about those situations now? Are you still vividly remembering them or have they faded with time?

I once had a boss who I disliked. My co-workers and I complained often about his incompetence and frustrating actions. My anger grew with each poor decision he made and it was a struggle to even be polite to him. After a time, he left our company, and I no longer had to deal with him. Years later when I ran into him unexpectedly, I was cordial and friendly. My anger toward him had progressed to resentment, but had not hardened into bitterness. After this boss was removed from my life, my resentment faded and I had no reason to wish him ill. He was not affecting my job any longer, and I rarely thought about him. My feelings had not progressed all the way to bitterness in this situation.

Jesus' Reactions to Offenses Against Him

Most of us become angry in similar types of situations. Things like being disagreed with, imposed upon, or betrayed by a friend will often incite anger. When we are inconvenienced and don't get our way or somehow feel unappreciated, we can erupt. If we are trying to help someone, and they rebuff our efforts, it can lead to indignation, a sense of injustice.

Jesus experienced these situations (and worse) but did not react with sinful anger. Because His mission was so closely aligned with God's will, He reacted only in righteous anger to offenses against God's law. There was no room for experiencing hurt feelings or being personally offended.

There was constant opposition in Jesus' earthly ministry. He was speaking out against the religious leaders who held power and prestige. They were jealous of His popularity, offended by His message, and fearful of His growing influence. For these reasons, they took every opportunity to argue with or discredit Jesus.

19. The things that Jesus endured would certainly cause you or me to be angry! Look up the following verses and list the ways Jesus was persecuted by the Jewish leaders.

Matthew 9:34:

Matthew 21:23:

Mark 12:14-15:

Luke 15:2:

Luke 16:14:

Luke 20:20:

John 8:13:

John 8:48:

20. And then there were instances where the people Jesus was ministering to were ungrateful and unkind. Read and describe these.

Matthew 14:12-13:

Matthew 15:22-28:

Mark 3:20:

Mark 8:1-3:

John 7:20:

John 10:20:

21. Jesus' own disciples misunderstood Him at best, and at worst didn't believe Him. They were not always loyal and often weak. He was ultimately betrayed to death by one. Here are some instances of this, read and note Jesus' reactions.

Matthew 26:48-50:

Mark 10:35-37:

Mark 14:34-37:

John 20:24-28:

John 21:17:

22. Even Jesus' own relatives were not sure what He was up to. He went from being a carpenter in their obscure little village to traveling the country and drawing crowds. They weren't convinced of His identity or calling and were embarrassed by Him. They thought He had lost His mind and believed they should intervene. Describe what they said about Him and any reaction Jesus had.

Matthew 12:47-50:

Mark 3:21:

Mark 6:2-4:

John 7:5:

23. And finally, when Jesus was crucified there were multiple instances of injustice. From the illegality of the Jewish trial to the manipulation of the crowds, there were many times when we could easily cry, "It's just isn't fair!" Even Pilate found no guilt in Jesus (John 19:4) but would not oppose the will of the angry mob. Surely you and I would react with some fury or self-pity. Maybe we would threaten retribution from God! But what was Jesus' reaction to this tragic miscarriage of justice?

Matthew 26:67-68:

Mark 14:61:

Mark 15:27-32:

Luke 23:28:

Luke 23:34:

Luke 23:43:

Jesus was human and knew what agony He faced leading up to the cross. He was deeply grieved and upset about the ordeal that was to come. He spent hours on His knees, pouring out His heart to Father God. John 12:27-28 recounts His sorrow and earnest prayers:

Now my soul is troubled, and what shall I say? 'Father, save me from this hour'? No, it was for this very reason I came to this hour. Father, glorify your name! (NIV)

Paul E. Miller, in *A Praying Life*, says of this passage,

> *Jesus was aware of his feelings but did not wallow in them. His soul was troubled but he submitted to God. Our culture makes feelings absolute. If you*

feel something, you must then act on it. Jesus dies to his own desires and worships the Father.

Jesus is our perfect example in every way. In the face of the most cruel and unfair treatment, He spoke words of love and forgiveness, not anger. How should we respond to offenses against us? Model Jesus. He cried out to God but ultimately surrendered His own will. We must trust God and die to our own selfish desires when circumstances are hard. Jesus' concern was ultimately for God's kingdom and purposes, not His own personal agenda.

Anger was created by God and intended for good. Anger's purpose is to prevent or stop violations against God's laws and character and bring restoration and healing in those circumstances. Jesus modeled righteous anger while on earth and did not ever succumb to selfish or sinful anger, even though there were many instances where He was insulted and provoked.

Application questions:

A. What things, people, or circumstances most often cause me to become angry? Is it usually for the same types of provocations?
B. What are the motivations behind my anger? Do expectations or hurt feelings contribute?
C. How can I specifically ask God to work in my heart so that I won't react in anger as often? In what areas do I need to grow?

Be not angry that you cannot make others as you wish them to be, since you cannot make yourself as you wish to be. ~ Thomas à Kempis

Lesson 2: When Bad Things Happen

Often the work of the Lord itself may be a temptation to keep us from that communion with Him which is so essential to the benefit of our own souls. ~ George Müller

Many of us had upbringings that were not ideal because our parents, siblings, and other friends or relatives were sinners. Some of us experienced grievous hurt, neglect, or abuse. It's easy to look at the world around us and become discouraged. Evil abounds, people are greedy and cruel. We see pain and injustice, and it's easy to ask, "Where is God?" or "Why didn't He prevent this from happening?"

Others grew up relatively unscathed only to discover later in life that people can disappoint us and the world is often a harsh place.

Blaming Others

Dysfunctional families and broken relationships are nothing new. The Bible is full of stories of unkind parents and jealous siblings.

Read the story of Joseph and his brothers in Genesis 37.

1. Did Joseph's brothers have reason to hate him? What were his offenses against them (from their viewpoint)?

2. What were their sins against him?

3. How did the brothers sin against their father, Jacob?

4. How did Jacob's actions contribute to the animosity among the brothers?

5. Read pp. 144-145 in *Bitter Truth*. How did Joseph ultimately respond to the sins committed against him by his brothers?

How we respond to wrongs committed against us often varies. Most of the time, our initial reaction is sinful anger and an accompanying action such as fighting back, hurtful words, or plotting revenge.

Sometimes the anger is directed inward, and we blame ourselves or believe we deserved poor treatment. Joseph had many years to think about what he had done and how his brothers had harmed him. I'm sure he did lots of soul-searching while forgotten in an Egyptian prison and came to the conclusion that he had at least *somewhat* provoked his brothers to their actions. He was not completely blameless in this scenario, although he certainly didn't deserve death or slavery. Things went from bad—slavery, but in a prosperous household—to worse, falsely accused and imprisoned. Still, his faith and trust in God ultimately did not waver.

6. Rephrase what Joseph told his brothers in Genesis 50:20.

Think of situations in your growing up years (or more recently) when you were harmed or unfairly treated.

7. How did you respond or react to these sins against you? Were any of your responses sinful?

8. What were some of the consequences or results of their sin (and if applicable, yours)?

It's easy, and perhaps natural, to sin when we're experiencing pain. The hurt is real and the wounds are deep. Some of our reactions may be:

- "How can I help but *do this* or *be this way* after what I've gone through?"
- "Why didn't I have the advantages others have had? God must not love me."
- "God can't expect me to be kind, loving, or unselfish when I have to protect myself. I have to make sure I'm not hurt like that again. I can't bear any more pain."

The sad truth is that sinful anger always leads to more sin. We sin because people sin against us. *Hurting people hurt others.* We respond in anger to their sin, and they then retaliate at an even greater level. Left unchecked, the situation can grow and escalate until there is open hostility or outright violence.

Read the section titled *Consider Paul* on pp. 145-147 in *Bitter Truth*.

9. How does Paul describe his dealings with Alexander the metalworker?

10. What was Paul's response to those who did not support him?

11. What does Paul say he is willing to endure and why (2 Timothy 2:9-10)?

Anger Toward God

The book of Job is a lesson for us in how to respond when the trials we face seem to have come straight from God's hand. He lost his children, all his wealth and possessions, and eventually his own health. When we suffer illnesses, natural disasters, or the death of someone we love, we can't rightly blame any person for causing them. These situations are God's doing, and we may become angry that He allowed or didn't prevent these things from happening.

Read Chapter 16, pp. 138-143 in *Bitter Truth* and review the story of Job.

12. How did Job respond to his tragedies in Job 1 and 2?

13. What caused him to change his tune?

14. What did Job accuse God of?

15. How did he respond after God's rebuke?

16. Can we be forgiven for being angry at God?

Who God Is

Theologian and pastor A. W. Tozer said, "What comes into our minds when we think about God is the most important thing about us" (*The Knowledge of the Holy, 1965*).

The way we understand God, who we truly believe Him to be, colors every event in our lives; past, present and future. If we reflect on our story without an accurate God-perspective, we may be tempted to feel anger or guilt, to assign blame to others, or to have regrets. How we respond to harmful offenses inflicted by others often depends upon our view of and faith in God. If we concentrate on the wrongs done to us or the ways we failed, it's easy to believe the lie that we are disqualified for the Lord's work. We may think of ourselves as sitting on the sidelines, watching the *good people* carry on the mission of the Kingdom. Only when we view our lives and the past hurts through the lens of who God can we see our story correctly.

God is the ultimate and perfect recycler. Nothing is wasted in His economy. He takes tragedy, sin, and failure, and makes it work toward His good purposes. He uses sinners and failures like you and me and the Apostle Paul!

Read 1 Timothy 1:12-17.

17. How does Paul describe himself?

18. Despite this, what does he say was given to him?

19. How does Paul describe Jesus in 1 Timothy 1:16?

20. How can we construct an accurate view of God?

TRUTH 1

GOD IS—good. He is *for* us, and He loves us. He is working all things for our good and His glory.

When we say God is good, we are saying there is nothing bad about Him. There is nothing in His character that has a hint of evil or malice. God has no dark side, no hidden motives, and He absolutely cannot sin. He is the only one in the universe this can be said about, which is a trait of His uniqueness, His *other*-ness, His holiness.

21. Read and summarize 1 John 1:5 and Psalms 5:4.

22. What does God *not do* (according to Numbers 23:19)?

23. Psalm 86:8 and Isaiah 46:9 say what about God?

24. What did Jesus say about God in Mark 10:18?

Our problem is that sometimes we think we are the ones who can define the term *good*. But what if what I define as *good* is what someone else sees as *bad?* Whose judgement is superior? And is there an absolute authority that teaches us how we may evaluate things?

Yes. God is the only One worthy to be the judge and the only standard of holiness and goodness. Dr. Wayne Grudem, author of *Systematic Theology: An Introduction to Biblical Doctrine*, writes, "The goodness of God means that God is the final standard of good, and all that God is and does is worthy of approval."

24. Romans 8:28 in the ESV says that for those who _____God,

all things work together for _____ , for those who _____

_____.

We must pay attention to what this verse *isn't* saying. It's not a general platitude of "everything works out for the best." It applies only to those who love God and are called according to His purpose; that is, children of God. Those who believe in Jesus and are trusting Him for salvation can claim this verse as a promise. If we are followers of Christ, we have this certainty that *whatever* happens, God is working for our good. When we suffer tragedy, it does not look like any sort of good at that moment. But we can cling to this promise: God is surely doing something *good,* perhaps beyond what we can see or understand right now.

So if you are God's beloved child, then this promise applies to you!

25. Let's continue to the next verse, Romans 8:29 in ESV. What is God's purpose in all of these things?

For those whom He foreknew (us) He also_____ to be

_____ to the image of His Son (Jesus Christ) , in order that He

might be the _____ among many brothers.

26. What does this mean? (Continue reading to verse 30, and look up in other translations if necessary.)

Continue reading Romans 8 to the end of the chapter, verses 31-39.

27. Summarize what God is doing in and for us, and what He has promised us:

Does God let bad things happen to His children because He is mean and vindictive? Is God *for* or *against* us?

28. Read 2 Corinthians 1:20. What are God's promises to us in Christ?

29. Read the verses before and after verse 20. What do you think this means?

We need to let this sink in and believe it in our deepest heart of hearts. God's purposes are for our good and His glory. He loves us, is for us, and is interceding for us. Nothing in all of the universe can separate us from His love or get in the way of His care for us.

Not a single thing or event. Not any person. Not even ourselves.

This is truth.

TRUTH 2

GOD IS—our Healer, our Helper, our Redeemer. He forgives and restores the ruined places and brings beauty from the ashes.

Read Luke 4:16-21. Jesus was reading from Isaiah 61, where His mission statement was summarized.

30. Study Isaiah 61:1-4 and use verbs to describe Jesus' mission—what He came to earth to do.

We are promised _____ and _____ instead of mourning. (Isaiah 61:2-3)

We are promised _____ instead of ashes. (Isaiah 61:3)

We are promised _____ instead of a spirit of despair. (Isaiah 61:3)

We can never look at our lives and say, "It's too late. I've made too many mistakes. God could never use me now."

Be assured, even if some consequences of your bad choices are permanent, God can still redeem those and restore all the broken pieces. We are told that God honors a contrite heart and a repentant spirit (Psalm 51:17). Remember He is working all things for our good and His glory.

Read Psalm 103:1-6.

31. What benefits does the Lord give us in these verses?

32. Read and paraphrase Psalm 147:1-3:

Isaiah 30:15 says that in _____ and _____ is our salvation. The rest of Isaiah 30 describes what will happen when His people repent.

Isaiah 30:26 tells us the Lord will bind up the _____ of His people and

_____ the wounds He inflicted (as punishment or consequences of sin).

33. In John 14:16-18, 26-27, Jesus promises to send a Helper. Describe Him and what He does for us.

TRUTH 3

GOD IS—Creator, all powerful, and in charge of the beginning and the end. He rules the universe and has sovereignty over all things. There is nothing too hard for Him.

34. Look up the definition of *sovereign* in the dictionary and write it below.

The Apostle John had a vision of Jesus in Revelation 1:12-18. Even though John was the "disciple Jesus loved" and they had been close while He was on earth, John's reaction in Revelation 1:17 was to _____ at His feet as though _____.

35. What would have caused this reaction?

36. How does John describe Jesus?

37. What terms does Jesus use to describe Himself?

38. Jesus tells John that He holds the keys to _____ and _____.

39. Think about the implications of this. What events does Jesus have control over? Is there anything He does *not* have charge of?

He is *The Living One*, in charge of life and death, heaven and hell. He has all power, all authority, all wisdom. And yet, Jesus puts His hand on John and reassures him, saying, "Don't be afraid." What tender care Jesus demonstrates for His friend, even in the midst of His frightening appearance and display of majestic power.

40. Read 2 Chronicles 6:30 and describe what Jesus has knowledge of.

41. What can we hide from Him?

42. How is God described in Psalm 86:8?

Read Job 37.

43. What does God's voice sound like?

44. What weather elements does God control?

44. How does God show His love (verse 13)?

45. The Almighty is _____ and exalted in _____ (verse 23).

Read Job 38:4-40:2. God is asking questions of Job.

46. What are the obvious answers to all of these questions?

47. What qualities of God are you impressed with in this passage?

TRUTH 4

GOD IS—compassionate, kind, and long-suffering toward us. He knew we couldn't save ourselves, which is why Jesus came to die for our sins and reconcile us to God.

48. Look up the following verses and list how God is described.

Exodus 22:27:

Psalm 25:6-7:

Psalm 86:7:

Psalm 86:15:

Psalm 116:5:

Psalm 145:8:

Luke 6:36:

James 5:11:

49. What characteristics of God lead us to repentance according to Romans 2:4?

50. Romans 5:8 in NIV tells us that God demonstrated His _____

because while we were still _____, Christ died for us.

51. How Romans 5:6 describes us?

52. How does Romans 5:10 label us?

53. And finally, what does Romans 5:11 call us? (Look this up in several different versions, see the NLT version especially.)

54. What does Jesus say we are in John 15:14-15?

Read the story in Matthew 14:10-14.

55. What had just happened and how did Jesus probably feel?

56. What did Jesus try to do?

57. How did He react in verse 14 to the crowds who followed Him?

58. How does God look upon us according to Psalm 103:11-14?

59. Read Ephesians 2:4-9. What did God do for us and what did we contribute ourselves?

These four truths should sustain us when we are in the middle of real life, with real problems. It's easy to take our eyes off God and instead focus on ourselves and our situations. But when that happens, we must remind ourselves of the truth and apply it accordingly.

List some circumstances in your life you are currently troubled about, or something that consumes a lot of your thinking.

Here are some I've had, just to get you thinking:

- My job is awful, my boss treats me unfairly.
- I don't see how we'll ever pay for our child's college education.
- My health issues.

60. What are yours?

If we are constantly worried or complaining about the challenges in our lives, it's the opposite of trusting God and surrendering to Him. It's a lack of faith. It's essentially another way of saying, "Lord, I don't know what You're doing here, I'm not sure You've got this. I don't believe you can bring about my good and Your glory through this situation. It's just too difficult." Most of us wouldn't actually dare say that *out loud* to God, but some might.

61. Read Mark 9:17-18, 21-22. What was the difficult situation this father faced with his son?

62. What did Jesus call him and the others observing the situation (Mark 9:19)?

63. How did Jesus admonish him (Mark 9:23)?

64. How did the father ultimately respond to Jesus (Mark 9:24)?

65. Do you think Jesus was pleased with his response? (Reference Hebrews 11:6.)

Application Questions:

A. How should we respond when people hurt us? How did the Apostle Paul model this?
B. Will you make a choice right now to release the cares you listed above to the One who is all-powerful, loving, and on your side?
C. Do you trust God to work out these circumstances for your good and His glory?

D. Will you choose to believe that your compassionate Heavenly Father cares about you and is interested in you?

Lesson 3: Recognizing Bitterness

Bitterness remembers only what it chooses to, and puts a negative spin on those events. ~ from Bitter Truth

And now for the fun part—how to identify bitterness in others and diagnose it in ourselves. I'm kidding. This is **not at all fun**. In fact, it can be embarrassing and painful to realize that we exhibit these traits. No one wants to come face to face with their own sin, but it is a necessary step. If we don't see the flaw, how can we ask God to change us?

None of us in our own strength has the power to affect lasting change. That's the work of the Holy Spirit. And praise God, He *does* the work when we invite Him into our hearts and lives. So, dear friend, remember that this may be tough, but it allows God to convict us if necessary.

Read the definition of bitterness on pp. 48-50 in *Bitter Truth*. Write a summary in your own words.

Food for Thought: Were you surprised by these definitions? What stood out to you the most?

Skim through Chapter 9 in *Bitter Truth,* pp. 64-79. List the 13 characteristics of bitterness outlined in bold.

1. A bitter person _____

2. A bitter person uses _____

3. A bitter person will _____

4. A bitter person _____

5. A bitter person _____

6. A bitter person only accepts _____

7. A bitter person remembers _____

8. A bitter person is _____

9. A bitter person is _____

10. A bitter person desires _____

11. Bitterness can be _____

12. Bitterness rarely _____

13. A bitter person is_____

14. Go back to Lesson 1, p. 6, in this study and review the description of sinful, selfish anger. Which of these 13 characteristics heavily involve our anger?

15. Review p. 9 of Lesson 1 with the chart showing the progression from anger to violence. Which of these characteristics are most closely linked with resentment?

16. Divide the 13 characteristics of bitterness accordingly and list in the chart below:

Bitterness in our words	Bitterness in our thoughts	Bitterness in our actions

Bitterness In Our Words

The number of verses in the book of Proverbs that covers the tongue is amazing. Many chapters are full of multiple exhortations and warnings about our speech. One of my favorites is:

Death and life are in the power of the tongue, and those who love it will eat its fruits. (Proverbs 18:21)

My mouth has always been a problem. Have you ever said something and immediately wished you could suck it back into your mouth? I have, many times. Unkind, critical words are a sure symptom of bitterness.

17. What does Luke 6:45 say about the relationship between our hearts and our mouths?

Another trait is that we are unconcerned about how our words have hurt or wounded others. Proverbs 12:18a says: The words of the reckless pierce like swords. The definition of reckless: "utterly unconcerned about the consequences of some action; without caution; careless." Unfortunately, once you say something, *it's out there and you can't get it back.*

18. Look up these verses in Proverbs that describe the careless or reckless tongue. List the possible consequences described.

Proverbs 17:14:

Proverbs 17:19:

Proverbs 18:6:

Proverbs 18:7:

Proverbs 18:19:

(And these are from only *two* chapters of Proverbs!)

We need to remember the ruin and destruction that can follow when we say something that will start an argument or pick a fight. I like the analogy of letting the waters out of a dam. Once that wall is broken, it will take a very long time to repair it, and even then it may never be back to the way it once was. When we think that the dispute we are starting with our criticism or unkind words will be like a strong castle with iron bars, we should live in fear of the results. It will be very difficult, if not impossible, to break through that barrier later. It's no wonder that so many people caught up in bitterness have strained or broken relationships.

19. What description of the tongue is given in James 3:6a?

What can be the consequences according to James 3:6b?

Bitterness in our Thoughts

A bitter person is unhappy. If you meet someone who is overflowing with joy and gratitude, it's a sure sign that they are not struggling with bitterness. Bitter people are miserable, never satisfied, and can even find fault in a situation where someone is attempting to bless them. They don't appreciate the gift they've been given or the effort that was extended. They think it should have been done according to their preferences and their suggestions should have been followed. If only they had received this or that or it had been done or said in this certain way, they would be satisfied, they say. (But they surely wouldn't!)

20. What does Psalm 90:14 say will satisfy us?

Going along with this is the tendency to be critical and always find fault. Whatever has happened, they think it should have been done differently. A bitter wife can tell you in detail what her husband isn't doing for her and how he should be a better husband. A bitter single person sees everything as being designed for couples. A bitter employee thinks they would run the department far better than their incompetent boss. Whatever the situation is, a bitter person will point out how it could have and *should have* been done better. (Especially if *they* were in charge!)

21. What's really at the root of this tendency?

Another common trait of a bitter person is excellent recollection. This one recalls the details of the offense committed against them and rehearses it repeatedly in their mind. Our memories are never so sharp as when we're remembering someone's unkind words or how they betrayed us. We can recount entire conversations in detail when attempting to "prove" that a certain person is really the monster we've made him out to be. We have a flawless (or so we think) image in our heads of the events, and we replay them over and over. It's evidence that we are right, we are justified in our anger. Unfortunately, since these events stay so fresh in our minds, they can still cause deep pain, even years after they occurred.

22. Read 2 Peter 3:1-2. What are we told to recall?

What will stimulate us to wholesome thinking (or a sincere mind)?

One of the biggest, most obvious, couldn't-miss-it-even-if-you-tried, colossal traits of a bitter person is selfishness. This manifests itself in self-serving actions and attitudes, self-protection, and my personal favorite—self-pity. In my life, self-pity has been the quickest route to bitterness. Consequently, it scares me if I hear my thoughts going in that direction: "Poor me. I never get to....." or "I've never had.......like they do" or "No one appreciates all that I do around here." Do you ever find yourself going down that path? *Beware*. The fruit of this kind of thinking is discontentment and blaming others, which ultimately leads to anger. And, as we've already said, anger is the doorway to bitterness.

• I blame my husband for not taking me on the exotic vacations I've dreamed of.
• I blame my parents for not fostering close family ties.
• I blame my grown children for not giving me enough attention or disappointing me in other ways.
• I blame God for not giving me what I desire: good health, close family relationships, success, money.
• I blame my boss for not promoting me or giving me a bonus.
• I blame my friend for not including me in that fun activity.

I hope you see how these thoughts can take us to resentment and bitterness.

23. In what ways are you tempted toward self-pity?

Read the story of my struggles with Doug on pp. 41-44 and pp.135-136 in *Bitter Truth*.

24. What was the faulty thinking I was caught in?

25. What are ways selfishness and self-pity can contribute to bitterness?

Bitterness in our actions

One action that a bitter person often manifests is quickly losing their cool and displaying a temper, since they are easily provoked to anger. In the bitter person's mind, a huge pile of all the offenses you've committed has been built and this is just *one more example* of your indifference or insults against them. In their way of thinking, this is the final straw, so they blow up. Their anger seems perfectly understandable and reasonable to them; you have *always* done this or *always* been this way or *never* listened! Others may be surprised that the bitter person is so upset over a seemingly minor thing, but they don't know the whole story, how many times this has happened, and how much you've been hurt or offended. Bitterness has also been defined as having "emotional sunburn," which means the person is overly sensitive and interprets everything as a personal affront against them.

26. What does Proverbs 22:24-25 tell us about a hot-tempered person?

A bitter person blames others, but excuses their own actions. You might call this living in denial. All of their problems and trials are someone else's fault. It might be a difficult boss or a disinterested spouse or a neglectful friend. "*They* have wronged *me*," they would say, "but *I* have not contributed to this situation in any way." The bitter person will explain their unkind behavior as being reasonable or inevitable because of the other person's actions. "Yes, I told everyone in the office how awful my boss is, but I *had* to so they will know to watch their backs," would be a rationale for gossip and slander. A woman may speak harshly to her husband, yet excuse it because "he needs to know how I feel" and she couldn't possibly keep it in, right? "That would be hypocritical!" she says.

One who is bitter will often say that *they couldn't help* how they reacted in that situation, it was only natural and understandable. There is no spotlight on their own evil words or actions, only an unrelenting focus on how others have wronged them and are to blame.

One who harbors bitterness desires vengeance (or an apology). When a bitter person is hurt or offended, they are intensely interested in appropriate "justice" or payback for their offender. They may seek to ruin a reputation, sever a relationship, or even cause bodily harm. You hear about crimes of passion, where someone's extreme anger boiled out of control and they committed murder. But reasonable and level-headed people like us just want an apology. When I was mired in bitterness, I sometimes daydreamed about the type of remorse I desired from the people who had wounded me. Of course, it never happened the way I wanted it to, so I continued to hang on to my resentment and anger. A bitter person may even reject a legitimate apology because it just wasn't right, not exactly what they wanted to hear, or wasn't truly sincere, or so they think.

27. What does Romans 12:19 say about revenge?

Lastly, our bitterness spreads and infects others. The sin of bitterness is called a "root" in Scripture (Hebrews 12:15). It spreads to others, especially in families. If I am holding on to resentment and unforgiveness toward someone, you can bet that my spouse and children will be influenced and will probably join me on my bitter bandwagon. I can persuade those in my workplace, church, or community group to hold a grudge or blame someone for an offense against me. I can cause division by spreading gossip or my version of "truth," which always paints the object of my bitterness in a bad light.

The tragic thing about most of these traits is that they allow no room for grace. Bitterness is ultimately grace-less.

28. Read Hebrews 12:15 and describe the consequences of the bitter root.

29. How important is grace in the life of a believer? Reference Ephesians 2:8-9 and John 1:16-17.

Application Questions:

A.   Which characteristics of bitterness seemed most familiar to you?

B. Did you recognize some of these tendencies in yourself?
C. Ponder God's grace toward us. Where would we be without it?

Lesson 4: Excuses, Obstacles, and Consequences

You will never reach your destination if you stop and throw stones at every dog that barks. ~ Sir Winston Churchill

After we explore this all thoroughly, we will finally move on to the good news. It's literally the *good news* of the gospel and God's love and mercy for us.

But first we have to understand the bad before we can get to the good. We must be warned against the effects of this insidious sin and understand what's at stake for our families, friends, and church communities. It's important to realize what we're up against and what keeps us from perhaps confronting our sin.

The first thing to remember is that our enemy desires to keep us deceived. He doesn't want us to think about or even realize that we are in sin. His strategy is to keep us distracted, focusing on our hurts or grievances and not about how we ourselves may be offending God.

1. How is our enemy described in 2 Corinthians 11:14 and 1 Peter 5:8?

2. How is he described in John 8:44 and Revelation 12:10?

3. What is the warning in Hebrews 3:13?

4. What strategies might he use to keep you from contemplating your own sin? If you were your enemy, what would you do to trip yourself up?

Common Excuses

Read through the first part of Chapter 15 in *Bitter Truth*, pp. 125-129. This section discusses common excuses that we can use for bitter words and actions. There are six of them, but I believe they can be boiled down to a basic three. (The others are regarding anger and hurt feelings and have already been discussed.)

Excuse 1: I'm not so bad; they are worse.

Excuse 2: They provoked or caused me to behave this way.

Excuse 3: I can't help it, it's just how I am.

Food For Thought: Think of times when you have excused your unkind words or actions in these ways.

Excuse 1: Comparing ourselves to others—it's easy to do this, especially when the other person is blatantly, obviously sinning. We think we look pretty good in comparison to them. After all, I only said *this*, not that. It could have been so much worse!

And this might be a legitimate excuse if God graded on a curve. But He doesn't. God is completely holy and righteous and cannot compromise His purity or tolerate sin.

5. Read Habakkuk 1:13. What does it tell us about God's attitude toward sin?

6. All sin is worthy of God's punishment. What does Romans 6:23a tell us about sin? What is its payment or *wages*?

Imagine God's response if we pled our case by saying, "So here's what I said and did, but I certainly was no Hitler!"

Excuse 2: I was provoked or led into sin. Others are to blame, not me.

The very first humans, Adam and Eve, reacted this way when caught in their sin. Read Genesis 3:12-13.

7. Who did Adam blame when God confronted him?

8. Who did Eve blame when God spoke to her?

9. Did God accept their excuses? How did He respond?

10. How did they still bear the consequence of their sin?

Our experiences do shape us, and we may be tempted to certain sinful behaviors as a result of childhood environments. Those who are subjected to abuse in childhood often face greater inclinations to similar behavior. Those who are abused sexually can be tempted to promiscuity or using pornography. Those who are abused physically can be prone to rage or violence. If you grew up in an angry or resentful family, you may certainly be more disposed to bitterness.

But being sinned against is not an excuse for sinful behavior. God is the Healer, and He is working out His own good purposes in our lives. He can redeem even the worst circumstances. We must run to Him for healing and the power to resist sin and not make excuses.

11. Who might you be tempted to blame for your sin?

Excuse 3: I can't help it, it's just how I am.

This was absolutely true—before Jesus came. We are all sinners (Romans 3:23) and cannot help ourselves. In fact, we are worse than we even believe.

12. How are we described in Jeremiah 17:9?

13. Read Romans 6:16-17. Before Christ rescued us, what was our relationship to sin? What power did we have to fight sin?

But now… read Romans 6:11-14.

14. Since we have been brought from death to life, what is our relationship to sin?

If this is true for you, you can no longer say that you "can't help it." Jesus *will help you help it* when you ask Him to. His power in us is what overcomes sin.

15. According to Ephesians 1:19-20, what is the power we have to resist sin?

How Our Sin Affects Those Around Us

16. Skim over Chapter 11 in *Bitter Truth*, pp 88-99. The section headings list 9 consequences of bitterness. List them and describe them briefly.

-

-

-

-

-

-

-

-

-

Sometimes it's easier to recognize problems if we first look at the results. These are the consequences of bitterness.

Are any of these true in your life right now?

Asking Yourself Tough Questions

A. What's your legacy?

A legacy is the heritage you pass on; the traditions or example you set, the effect you will have on the generations to come. It's the environment you create with your attitudes and habits.

What's the legacy you are establishing now for your family, friends, co-workers, and church family? What is the aroma you leave behind?

Review p. 96 in *Bitter Truth* about my bitter family legacy.

Is there anyone in your family or church that you are not currently speaking to?
Is there someone that you could reach out to? Is there a division that you could help restore or mend?

Imagine your own funeral, hopefully many years from now. What do you want your children to say about you? How about siblings or other extended family members?

Do you think your desires are realistic based on your current relationship status? Are there circumstances you have the power to influence for good?

17. What guidance does Luke 6:27-28 and Romans 12:17-18 give for strained relationships?

18. In Ephesians 4:31-32, there are admonitions for holy living. What are they and could they be used to describe you?

Read the story of Abigail and David in 1 Samuel 25:2-35.

19. Did Abigail react the same as her husband?

20. What was David's compliment to her (v. 33)?

21. What was Abigail's ultimate legacy? Was it the same as her husband's?

B. Are you a fountain or a drain?

A fountain pours out cool, refreshing water. Do you water, bless, and nourish others with your words and actions? Do you demonstrate joy and hope? Do you point people to Christ and offer to pray for and with them? Does what pours out of your mouth provide refreshment and encouragement to those around you?

22. Use a thesaurus to find synonyms for the word *encourage* and write them below.

Food for Thought: Are these traits people would assign to me?

Are you a fountain, or are you a drain? Do you suck the positive feelings from the room with complaining and griping? Do people expect negativity or argument from you? Is your main topic of conversation *yourself?* Might you be considered quarrelsome? Are you considered a glass-half-full or a glass-half-empty kind of person? Do you more closely resemble Winnie the Pooh or Eeyore?

23. List the effects of a quarrelsome person as described in Proverbs 26:21 and Proverbs 27:15.

Death and life are in the power of the tongue, and those who love it will eat its fruits.
(Proverbs 18:21 ESV)

In the last lesson, we discussed the negative effects of the tongue. But let's remember the other side of this verse. There is also the power of *life* in what we say.

What was the last compliment you received? What was the last genuine pat on the back you gave to someone else? It's easier for me to remember the negative things said to me than the positive ones. I must choose to remember the kind, encouraging remarks of others that were meant to build me up. I must also remind myself to dispense kind words liberally to others. It will motivate life within them!

24. Look up Proverbs 16:24 in the NLT. The word "encourage" means to literally give courage to someone else. We can remind them of hope, direct them to Jesus. We can point out the good things we see the Lord doing in them and push them to persevere. We can set an example of thankfulness and talk about the blessings we have all received.

My desire is to speak words that give life, not death. How about you?

C. Do you have joy?

Most of the consequences of bitterness are the opposite of joy. If you feel alienated from God and others, you won't have His joy. We are told in Psalm 16:11 that in His presence is *fullness of joy.* A close, intimate relationship with our good and kind Father God necessarily produces joy. And we know that sin blocks the intimacy we desire and dampens our relationship.

Joy is also a fruit of the Holy Spirit who lives in us as believers.

25. List the fruits of the Spirit as described in Galatians 5:22-23.

26. Go back and review the consequences of bitterness again. Which are in direct contrast to the Spirit's fruit?

Joy doesn't come from happy circumstances or necessarily smooth sailing. Review the story of Paul and Silas in Philippi (Acts 16.) After they were "severely flogged" and thrown into prison (v. 23), they kept the other prisoners awake at midnight (v. 25) by singing hymns of praise! I don't know about you, but if I were beaten and thrown into prison, my first instinct would *not* be to sing praise songs! But Paul and Silas possessed true joy in the Lord and had great influence in that jail, resulting in the jailer's conversion and his entire family.

This is the kind of joy I want that rejoices in God's goodness even in hard circumstances. The kind that makes an impact on others when they see how we react to difficulty. The genuine joy that comes from being in His presence.

One Final Obstacle

What if the sin against you is not only unkind or unfair treatment, but an actual crime? Shouldn't you demand justice?

Yes. If you have been robbed or assaulted or harmed, you should prosecute the offense. The police should be called, and the perpetrator should be found and punished.

Christians have sometimes been counseled to just forgive the offender and not press charges, especially in situations of abuse within a church. But this is not biblical. The role of government is to punish criminals and protect society from crime.

> *For the one in authority is God's servant for your good. But if you do wrong, be afraid, for rulers do not bear the sword for no reason. They are God's servants, agents of wrath to bring punishment on the wrongdoer. (Romans 13:4 NIV)*

The problem can arise after justice has been served through human agencies. My desire to see "my version of justice" done in this situation can feed feelings of resentment or bitterness. If I believe the punishment was not appropriate or severe enough, I can seek to take vengeance into my own hands—or just obsess about it and stew in anger. We are warned against this in Romans 12:19:

> Do not take revenge, my dear friends, but leave room for God's wrath, for it is written: "It is mine to avenge; I will repay," says the Lord. (NIV)

27. How should we respond if a criminal is not punished or not punished harshly enough in our opinion?

Ultimately, we must remember that God is the Judge. He sees every thought and action and His justice will be perfect and fair.

28. How should we respond to criminals? See Matthew 5:44, Matthew 25:36, and Hebrews 13:3.

We've heard stories of those who forgave their offenders, befriended them in prison, and later led them to Christ. God can do the impossible!

Application Questions:

A. Are any of the consequences of bitterness apparent in your life?
B. What legacy will you leave behind?
C. Would others call you a fountain or a drain?
D. Do you possess genuine joy? What does it look like?

No one is ever united with Jesus Christ until he is willing to relinquish not sin only, but his whole way of looking at things. To be born from above of the Spirit of God means that we must let go before we lay hold, and in the first stages it is the relinquishing of all pretense. ~ Oswald Chambers

Lesson 5: The Gospel — How Much We Are Loved

Unbelief is safe, because it takes no risk and almost always gets what it expects. ~ Bill Johnson

The term *Christian* (First used at Antioch, Acts 11:26) is what we call someone who is *of* Christ, who follows Christ as a lifelong commitment. Other terms commonly used are saved, born again, converted, become a child of God, disciple, and believer. However, in our world today, Christian has become a rather generic term. It often only distinguishes someone who is not a Jew or a Muslim.

For our purposes, I'll use the term *believer* because it means one who *believes* (in Jesus and His message) versus someone who does not.

> *Therefore, if anyone is in Christ, he is a new creation. The old has passed away; behold, the new has come. (2 Corinthians 5:17 ESV)*

Believer is also a good term because it implies action and lifestyle. If you are a believer in the benefits of healthy eating, you probably don't consume junk food. If you believe that the office chair is sturdy and will hold your weight, you will sit in it every day. We vote for a particular law or candidate because we believe they will accomplish good things. What we believe in causes us to act.

So what is this message of Jesus that we either believe or disbelieve? Many times it's called the gospel, which literally means "good news."

Chapter 12 in *Bitter Truth* gives the basic gospel message. Read through pp.103-107.

1. Summarize in your own words what the gospel is.

How It Happens

2. According to Ephesians 2:4-5, what does God contribute to the process (of us becoming saved)?

3. Read Ephesians 2:8-9. What does it say about our role in the salvation process?

4. What is God's role?

5. What is essential to possess in order to please God (see Hebrews 11:6)?

6. Where do we get it?

7. What else does Ephesians 2:13-14 say that God did for us?

8. How can you respond to someone who thinks they become right with God through their good works?

What To Do

9. How is the process of salvation described in these verses?

Mark 16:16:

John 3:3:

John 3:15-18:

John 5:24:

Acts 16:31:

Romans 4:3:

Romans 10:9:

10. Do any of these passages mention a specific prayer, ritual, or formula?

11. If a person has heard and understood the gospel, what does it take for them to be saved? What elements are essential in obtaining salvation?

12. What does James 2:19 say about the demons?

13. What is the difference between them and a true believer?

What We've Now Received

As a believer in Christ, we have received life when we deserved only death. We were orphans and are now beloved children. We have received every spiritual blessing in Christ and grace upon grace. We have so much to be thankful for and rejoice in. Let's examine some of the benefits of our salvation in more detail. In Christ, we have received:

A. Righteousness

14. What do we become in Christ, according to 2 Corinthians 5:21?

In Revelation 19:6-9, there's a description of the Wedding Feast of the Lamb and His Bride (Jesus and us).

15. Verse 8 says we will receive fine white linen to wear, which is:

B. Forgiveness

16. Read Hebrews 8:12. What sins of ours will He remember?

Write out Ephesians 1:7 here.

17. What is our forgiveness dependent upon or *according to*?

18. What is there a total absence of? See Romans 8:1 and Isaiah 51:22.

C. The Holy Spirit

19. God the Holy Spirit dwells inside believers and provides a multitude of benefits. Read the following verses and place them in the proper column in the chart. Some might be applicable to more than one:

2 Corinthians 1:22, Galatians 4:6, John 14:26, John 15:26, John 16:7-8, 1 Corinthians 2:11-13, 1 Corinthians 6:19, 1 Corinthians 12:7, Titus 3:5-6, Acts 1:8, Acts 5:32, Romans 5:5, Romans 8:6, Romans 8:11, Romans 8:14, Romans 8:26.

Helper	Teacher	Giver	Comforter
		a pledge, a seal 2 Cor 1:22	

Who We Are — Our Identity

Who were we before and who are we now?

20. According to Ephesians 2:19:

21. According to John 15:15:

22. What else are we called? See Galatians 3:26.

It's easy for me to forget these truths, so I've created a little acronym to help remember who I am in Christ. It's not perfect, but it works! I hope it will help you believe truth when you are tempted to forget who you are. It's ABC—ARF. :-)

A - Adopted. I'm adopted into God's family (Ephesians 1:5). Adoption takes time, money, and great effort. Adopted children are desperately wanted, and God desired for me to become His child, so He made the way possible through Christ.

B - Blessed. Ephesians 1:3 says we are "blessed with every spiritual blessing in Christ." Every means *every*. What do we lack? Nothing. We are abundantly blessed from the graciousness of our Heavenly Father.

C - Chosen. Ephesians 1:4 says He chose us before the creation of the world. We were thought of and known before the beginning. The end of verse 4 adds the phrase "in love." This choice originated from God's great love for you and me.

A - Accepted. Ephesians 1:6 in the King James version says "accepted in the beloved." We are not rejected by God, because we are acceptable in His beloved Son. God is not disappointed in us or thinking about casting us off. We belong to Him!

R - Redeemed. We have been redeemed, or rescued from the kingdom of darkness. We don't need to fear death, and we are not slaves to sin any longer. We've been ransomed at great cost by our Brother, Friend, and Savior.

F - Forgiven. Ephesians 1:7 speaks of our forgiveness. The debt we owed and could never repay has been fulfilled. The slate has been wiped clean.

And all of these things are motivated by God's great love for us!

Read and ponder 1 John 3:1-2 in NIV.

23. See what great love the Father has _____ on us, that we should

be called _____ of God.

You too are the one whom Jesus loves. That's who you are. You need to personalize that until it breaks through the pavement of your brain, sinks into the soil of your soul, and takes root and bears fruit. You are the one whom Jesus loves. The more you get it, the less you'll sin. Love is the great motivator on the pathway of purity. The more you know you are loved, the less you will want to trample on love. You are the one whom Jesus loves! ~ Dr. Rob Reimer from Pathways to the King

What We Produce

If we are the branches attached to the vine of Christ (see John 15:1-2), it is a natural result to produce fruit.

Jesus said:
You did not choose me, but I chose you and appointed you so that you might go and bear fruit—fruit that will last—and so that whatever you ask in my name the Father will give you. (John 15:16 NIV)

One definition of fruit is: anything produced or accruing; product, result, or effect; return or profit. (dictionary.com) Our lives are expected to look differently since we have the power of the indwelling Holy Spirit. God's grace within us must produce evidence.

24. Review again and list the fruits of God's Holy Spirit (Galatians 5:22-23).

25. Think of some specific examples or actions of fruit that a believer may produce.

26. What does Titus 2:11-12 say about the results of salvation?

27. What other exhortation for believers is given in 1 Peter 1:22?

28. How did John the Baptist warn the religious leaders of his time? See Matthew 3:8-10.

Application Questions:

A. Can I clearly articulate the gospel message to someone who asks?
B. As believers, what do we lack to fight and overcome sin?
C. What fruit is evident in my life today?

Our works do not generate righteousness, rather our righteousness in Christ generates works. ~ Martin Luther

Lesson 6: The Process of Overcoming

Many deaths must go into reaching our maturity in Christ, many letting goes. ~ Elisabeth Elliot

We once were slaves to sin, but no longer! Christ has set us free. Galatians 5:1 tells us: "It is for freedom that Christ has set us free. Stand firm, then, and do not let yourselves be burdened again by a yoke of slavery."

1. What kind of slavery is this verse referring to?

We are not slaves to sin, no matter how fiercely we are tempted or how often we have failed in the past. Through Christ we are triumphant, victorious overcomers.
1 John 5:4 says, "…for everyone born of God overcomes the world. This is the victory that has overcome the world, even our faith."

And, again as a reminder—

2. What power is in us through the Holy Spirit? Read Ephesians 1:19-20.

Where to Start? Repent and Confess

3. Read Chapter 14, pp.114-124 in *Bitter Truth*. List the 9 steps that are laid out in the process of overcoming sin and describe briefly.

#1

#2

#3

#4

#5

#6

#7

#8

#9

4. Can these steps be applied to *any* sin or just bitterness?

Let's examine each step in closer detail.

#1 - Repent.

What is repentance?
Dictionary.com defines it this way: deep sorrow, compunction, or contrition for a past sin, wrongdoing, or the like. Regret for any past action.

So repentance is to show remorse; we say and feel sorry for our actions. Then we express a desire to change, to be different, to do the right thing. These are the dictionary definitions, but they are also biblically accurate. Repentance, in a biblical sense, is also *agreeing* with God that what you have done is against His law and contrary to His commands.

One last definition of repentance is simply turning around and going the opposite way. To repent of one's choice is to make a different or alternate one.

So in this step we:
- Agree with God that what I've done is sin.
- Feel remorse and sorrow that I have failed and express a desire to act differently.
- Turn and move in the opposite direction.

Notice how personal, how self-focused this process is? However, we often try to include others and not make it only about us.

"But what about my tough circumstances?"

"What about those other people that were doing the same things, or worse?"

"Don't you see how I was provoked? That person drives me crazy!"

"How could anyone be expected to act righteously in this difficult situation?"

Our excuses are that our surroundings contributed to our sin, or peer pressure got the best of us, or somebody else started it. True repentance is all about *me*. It's about *my* reaction, *my* response, *my* personal decision to say or do a certain thing. I take responsibility, I own up to my fault. It doesn't matter what everyone around me did or that the situation was difficult and unfair. Repentance is truly and uniquely personal. I often imagine repentance as a glass tube between me and God; straight up to heaven, connecting me to Him.

5. What are some obstacles you face in truly repenting of your sin?

I was addicted to the hokey pokey, but I turned myself around. ~ Unknown

#2 - Choose to forgive those you are bitter against. We make the choice to forgive with the help of God's Holy Spirit. It's such a difficult topic that I've dedicated an entire lesson to it. We will cover it thoroughly in the Lesson 7.

#3 - Repeat 1 & 2. Repent, forgive, repent, forgive, repent, forgive…

Here's where the rubber meets the road, so to speak. Here's where it gets tough. Eugene Peterson refers to the process of being sanctified in the Christian life as "a long obedience in the same direction." It's not just a few steps, it's miles and days and years of plodding onward in the journey. This continual obedience can be summed up in one word—perseverance.

6. What does the Bible say about those who persevere? (James 1:12 and James 5:11)

7. According to these verses, what are the results of perseverance? In 1 Corinthians 13:7, what always perseveres?

8. What was Jesus' example of perseverance in Hebrews 12:1-3?

In my experience, the choice to repent of my sin and forgive others was gut-wrenchingly difficult. I knew it was the right thing, but it was so hard! And when I finally decided to trust God and do it, I felt freedom and release. At least at first. In the days following, it seemed to get harder and harder. All the rationales I had for *why my sin wasn't really sin* and how the people I needed to forgive *didn't deserve it at all* came back in full force. Every time I made the choice to repent and forgive, something would come up to anger or discourage me.

9. Why do you think this happened? Review 1 Peter 5:8.

Our enemy doesn't want us to repent and have victory. He wants to keep us trapped in sin and shame. He will definitely make efforts to hinder you and put obstacles in your path. It may get worse before it gets better.

10. What is the encouragement in 1 John 4:4?

Fortunately, we have others to help us along the way.

#4 - Ask for help and prayer.

11. Read James 5:13-16. It lists instances in which you should ask your spiritual leaders to pray for you. What are they?

12. What is the promise in verse 15?

#5 - Ask for accountability. Ask a friend or mentor to check in with you regularly. Give them permission to ask you tough questions and answer them honestly. Ask them to pray for you and with you. We were never meant to do battle all alone. We are given our Christian brothers and sisters to encourage us. As one of our pastors likes to say, "There are no Lone Ranger Christians!"

#6 - Pray for yourself. Ask God to change you. Ask for His help, for more of His Spirit.

13. What is the promise in John 3:34?

14. What are we commanded to do in Matthew 7:7-8?

15. From Luke 11:13, what are we promised to receive when we ask?

16. James 5:16b says that the prayer of a righteous person is:

#7 - Deal quickly with anger. Review Ephesians 4:26-28.

17. Verse 26 mentions anger, what is the warning?

18. Review Lesson 1 on Anger. It is often the _____ to bitterness.

The warning here is to not let our anger build up; we mustn't let it stew or fester in our minds or hearts.

19. Verse 27 warns us against what?

20. How could holding on to our anger result in this?

21. From p. 116 in *Bitter Truth,* what is the timeframe for letting go of our anger?

#8 - Fight in the battlefield of your mind. We must let our minds be transformed by Christ. This is a vast topic that we will cover comprehensively in Lessons 9 and 10.

#9 - Be patient. Don't give up at the first sign of failure. Remember to persevere. Change takes time; a cruise ship can't be turned on a dime! I spent many years wallowing in bitter thoughts and habits, and my mind didn't change overnight. But eventually, God established new thoughts and habits—His thoughts—and I have been changed! It does get easier over time; the battles get easier to fight with obedience and persistence.

God's Promises About Confession and Repentance

He Feels Compassion For Us

22. Read Psalm 103:8-10 and Joel 2:13. How is God described in these verses?

23. According to Romans 2:4, what leads us to repentance?

24. In Psalm 103:13-14, how does God describe us?

Jesus Helps Us When We Face Temptation

For this reason he had to be made like them, fully human in every way, in order that he might become a merciful and faithful high priest in service to God, and that he might make atonement for the sins of the people. Because he himself suffered when he was tempted, he is able to help those who are being tempted. (Hebrews 2:17-18)

25. Why is Jesus able to help us when we are tempted?

Read Hebrews 4:15-16. This is a beautiful picture of the High Priest who receives our humble confession and then forgives us and helps us in our need.

26. Did Jesus ever sin?

27. What awaits us at God's throne?

We're promised also in James 4 that when we repent and humble ourselves before the Lord, He will come to our rescue. The temptation will pass and we will be lifted up. Let's cling to this promise and choose once again to persevere in obedience.

Submit yourselves, then, to God. Resist the devil, and he will flee from you. Come near to God and he will come near to you. Wash your hands, you sinners, and purify your hearts, you double-minded. Grieve, mourn and wail. Change your laughter to mourning

and your joy to gloom. Humble yourselves before the Lord, and he will lift you up.
(James 4:7-10)

God Values Humility and Repentance

True repentance begins with humility, which is the opposite of pride. Pride says, "I've been wronged!" Humility says, "I am wrong."

God opposes the proud but shows favor to the humble. (James 4:6)

28. Who does God look upon with favor? See Isaiah 66:2.

29. What does God value, according to Psalm 51:17?

Living a life in submission to Christ means humbling myself again and again. Years ago when my kids were little, they sometimes avoided obeying. They would stall and use every delay tactic to evade getting ready for bed or picking up their toys. I often asked at that point, "Are you going to obey me or not?" When I presented the options as simply *yes* or *no*, they would finally comply.

That's really all it comes down to, isn't it? Will we obey Jesus or not? Yes or no? It's hard to obey and forgive someone over and over and over. It's hard to choose love when you want to lambast somebody with proof of how wrong they are. We think they need to understand the consequences of their actions and how much they are hurting us.

But this is pride and self-righteousness. How many times has Jesus forgiven me? How many times have I offended others and they have covered it over with love? How big is the debt that I've been forgiven?

Humility makes us recognize how weak and helpless we truly are. And that's when God's power is best on display.

30. "But we have this treasure in jars of clay to show that this all-surpassing power is from _____ and not from _____." 2 Corinthians 4:7 (NIV).

He's Changing Us

31. When we humble ourselves in repentance, what does God promise to do for us? (See 1 Peter 5:6.)

32. What gift does God give to the contrite in Isaiah 57:15?

33. Read and ponder Philippians 1:6. Who began and who will finish the work in us?

I love how Jeremiah 15:19 is translated in the NLT:

> This is how the Lord responds:
> "If you return to me, I will restore you
> so you can continue to serve me.
> If you speak good words rather than worthless ones,
> you will be my spokesman.
> You must influence them;
> do not let them influence you!"

This is what true repentance looks like. It's the practice of humility and being restored so that we may serve Jesus. Those who have been forgiven are gracious and merciful to others. May we influence others with our good words. May we produce the proof of repentance every day in our speech, actions, and reactions.

A Final Caution: What Happens If I Don't Repent and Forgive?

If you decide that you're *not* going to obey God by confessing your sin and forgiving others, here's what you may expect in the future:

• **An Increase in Pride**

Refusing to submit to God is evidence of pride. Pride is the voice that won't be told what to do, the one who thinks he doesn't need help. A prideful spirit says, "My way works for me." and "My secrets are nobody else's business."

God Hates Pride.
34. Summarize Proverbs 8:13 and Proverbs 16:18.

Pride Leads to Captivity. Read the warnings in Jeremiah 13:15-17.

35. The last part of verse 17 says the Lord's flock will be taken _____.

• **Increased Bondage to Sin**

If I persist in refusing forgiveness to those who have wounded me, I will grow a harvest of bitterness. This will turn me into a hard-hearted person and separate me from others. I will not have joy in my Christian walk. I will be more easily tempted to other sins. I will not be able to give or receive love. I will wallow in self-pity and blame everyone else for my loneliness and despair.

• **Increased Influence of the Enemy**

Our enemy wants to kill us and destroy our faith. By letting our anger fester and grow into bitterness, we are giving him more opportunity in our lives. Ephesians 4:27 says he gains a "foothold," which means a space, a perch, or a secure position in our hearts. This spot is a basis for further progress and influence over us. Sin, when given free reign, always leads to more sin.

In Contrast...

God desires to forgive us and heap blessings upon us when we repent. He desires to set us free and release us from the chains of sin in our lives.

36. Read Joel 2:22-27 and list the Lord's promise and kindnesses.

Application Questions:

A. Which of the 9 steps in overcoming is hardest for you?
B. How does God help us in the process of repentance?
C. Are there ways I'm struggling with humility?

The cultivation of a penitential spirit is absolutely essential to spiritual progress. ~ A.W. Tozer

Lesson 7: About Forgiveness

We all agree that forgiveness is a beautiful idea until we have to practice it. ~ C. S. Lewis

Read pp. 153-160 in *Bitter Truth*.

Fill in the blanks.

1. Forgiveness has a _____ while bitterness remembers
_____. (p.153)

2. *Charizomai* means to _____ which means I'm willing to

extend_____ even to my enemies with a view toward their

_____. (p.154)

3. Jesus teaches that loving our enemies is a _____. (p.155)

4. How many times should we forgive? (pp.156-157)

5. What is the main point of Matthew 18:23-35? (p.158)

Five Reasons To Forgive

A. We have been forgiven so much ourselves.

From the above passage (Matthew 18:23-35) we learn that God expects us to forgive in response to the lavish mercy and forgiveness we've received. We must review how vast is the love we've been given and how much mercy and forgiveness our loving Father has bestowed on us. We must remember the pain and separation of the cross; how much Jesus suffered to bring about our redemption. In the words of the hymn, "When I Survey the Wondrous Cross,"

> *Were the whole realm of nature mine,*
> *That were a present far too small;*
> *Love so amazing, so Divine,*
> *Demands my soul, my life, my all.*

6. Read Luke 7:47 and fill in:

Whoever has been forgiven_____.

B. Jesus tells us to.

If you are a follower and disciple of Jesus Christ, forgiveness is not an option. It's a direct command. No ifs, ands, or buts—there's no choice here. We must forgive those who offend or hurt us. The story of the unforgiving servant in Matthew 18:21-35 ends with a dire warning. The same threat is given in Matthew 6:14-15. The warning is that we ourselves will not be forgiven if we refuse to forgive.

7. Colossians 3:13 tells us to forgive _____.

8. Why does Mark 11:25 tell us to forgive?

C. It's a testimony to the world.

The act of forgiveness reflects God's heart and is such a foreign concept in our culture. We are like Him when we forgive and it sets us apart. We act and live differently as Christians; it's part of the proof of the Spirit's work in us.

In the story of *Les Misérables* by French author Victor Hugo, the convicted criminal Jean Valjean is persuaded to turn his life around and follow God because of the lesson of forgiveness. He steals valuables from a priest and is in danger of going back to prison for the rest of his life. Instead, the priest graciously offers him forgiveness which becomes the turning point for Valjean.

9. 1 Peter 3:9 tells us to repay evil with _____.

10. Matthew 5:44 says to _____ who persecute you.
D. God will defend us and punish evil.

Part of our faith in making this choice of obedience is trusting that God will bring about justice for sinners. Romans 12:19 says *"Beloved, never avenge yourselves, but leave it to the wrath of God, for it is written, 'Vengeance is mine, I will repay, says the Lord.'"*

11. What is the promise in 2 Thessalonians 1:6-7?

12. How is the Lord described in Psalm 3:3?

13. Read Lamentations 3:58-66 and describe what the Lord does for us.

E. It's good for us.

Doing things God's way is always going to bring us optimal peace and well-being. God created our minds and bodies, so surely He knows the healthiest way for them to function. Following is an excerpt from a blog post by a medical researcher:

"Why Forgiveness is Critical for Your Health"
by Stefani Yorges, Ph.D.
www.leadinghigher.com

The process of forgiving is one of the most exhausting struggles you will face, because the battle will involve both your mind and emotions. Maybe you have been mentally replaying the hurt for days, months, or even years. So you repeatedly experience the same anxiety, anger, and frustration. These are among the most toxic emotions a person can have, draining your energy and resources. Your heart cannot rest in this state and you suffer physical and emotional problems.

Medical professionals agree that many of our long-term illnesses come as a result of bitterness, unforgiveness, and emotional stress. Pent-up hostility and anger produce depression and anxiety, along with a host of physical problems.

Nearly 20 years of research at the University of Wisconsin showed that people who forgave had better psychological health. The studies revealed significant improvements in depression, anxiety, post-traumatic stress, self-esteem, and coping skills among those who were able to forgive.

What Forgiveness Is *Not*

- When I forgive someone for an offense, I am not condoning their actions or saying the actions weren't sin.

- When I forgive someone, I am not removing any consequences of the sin that may still occur.

- When I forgive someone, it doesn't make me their judge or confessor. I am not *better* than them. My forgiveness is in obedience to Christ and we will all stand before Him as equals.

- Forgiveness does not equal reconciliation. Hopefully, forgiveness is the first step toward reconciliation between two people, but it does take both parties. If only one has forgiven and the other has not, Romans 12:18 should be our guide.

14. Describe the instructions in Romans 12:18.

- When I forgive someone, I can't rely on my feelings as proof that I have forgiven. My feelings may not change immediately, but if I persevere in forgiveness and obedience, they will eventually catch up.

Which brings us to a question I've often been asked—

What If I Can't Forgive Myself?

The short answer: You have no power to forgive, only God can forgive.

But when someone says this, usually they are speaking of the lingering guilt they feel, which we can also call shame. Maybe they have asked God to forgive them, but they don't feel forgiven. They are weighed down with their sin and feel bad and unworthy all the time. There seems to be no solution.

First of all, let's review what God's Word says:

15. 1 John 1:9 says if we confess our sin, _____

_____.

16. Romans 8:1 says that if we are in Christ there is

_____.

17. What does the blood of Jesus do, according to Hebrews 9:14?

This is what God's Word says about us and our sin. It is truth.

So someone who still feels guilty and condemned after confessing their sin is not believing truth about the matter. They may be listening to other voices and influences.

Read Revelation 12:10.

18. Who is the accuser?

19. What does he do to our brothers and sisters?

20. What is his goal?

If you are constantly feeling accused and not forgiven of your sin, perhaps you are listening to the accuser.

Or perhaps your own feelings are guiding you to perpetual guilt.

21. 2 Corinthians 5:7 says we live by faith and not by _____.

Synonyms for the word *sight* include perception, appearance, view, and vision. Our sight is how we perceive or view the world. This could also influence our feelings. Because I see others who seem more righteous than me, I can convince myself that I'm sinful, unworthy, and not forgiven. This is trusting my feelings, perception, or sight.

We're told not to do this, but instead to live by faith. We must believe what God's Word says and not live by our feelings or impressions. I must choose to believe that what God says about me and my sin are true. I am forgiven!

The long answer (to what if I can't forgive myself?): Believe God. Trust His Word and not your own feelings. Don't listen to the voice of the enemy who wants to accuse you and leave you stewing in guilt and shame.

I think that if God forgives us we must forgive ourselves. Otherwise, it is almost like setting up ourselves as a higher tribunal than Him. ~ C. S. Lewis from The Collected Letters of C.S. Lewis, Volume 3

Steps To Forgive

Remember that forgiveness is really difficult. It's a seemingly insurmountable obstacle at times. There's a *reason* we didn't just let that offense go at first. It hurts, it's unfair, they shouldn't have done it.

I know I struggle to forgive when someone is simply rude or ungrateful. How can people forgive those who abuse them or steal from them or hurt their children!? But of course, I do know how they do it. With God, *nothing* is impossible. I have personally experienced this. Through the power of the Holy Spirit I was able to let go of grudges I had held on to for years. Jesus said it Himself in Mark 9:23: "*All things* are possible for one who believes." Through faith, you and I can forgive both a heinous crime and the slightly annoying oversight.

Before you get too discouraged and think, "Well, good for her. It doesn't work that way for me!" I believe it's impossible to forgive in our human strength without the power of the Holy Spirit within us. God doesn't give His children commands that are impossible to obey. He's not that kind of harsh, unreasonable Father. I think that these commands such as *love your enemies* and *forgive those who hurt you* are given to us so that God's power might be obviously apparent in our weakness. They go against the fabric of who we are, after all. In our human nature, we say it's not fair, and we clamor for revenge. We want payback or justice.

22. Review 2 Corinthians 12:9 and write it here:

1 Peter 1:3 says we've received *everything* we need for life and godliness. That means we have the power and the ability to forgive. We have received what we need to do this seemingly insurmountable thing—over and over and over.

23. What do we lack when it comes to the ability to forgive?

24. What does 2 Corinthians 9:8 promise us?

However, it is a choice. It's an act of our will. Yes, it's only possible through the power of God working in us, but we must choose to take the first step. It's a decision. I decide to give up my right to be angry and hurt. I decide to surrender my desires and obey Christ.

Forgiveness is an act of the will, and the will can function regardless of the temperature of the heart. ~ Corrie Ten Boom

Nancy Leigh DeMoss wrote *Choosing Forgiveness*. The book's title supports the idea that forgiveness is an action, a choice. We don't wait until we feel like forgiving (because that would likely never happen), we take the step, set the plan in motion. She says,

> "...if you are a child of God, you have been infused with the same power that He worked in Christ when He raised him from the dead (Ephesians 1:20) – think of that! So choose it! Do it! Don't wait to feel like it or to figure out how it will all work out. Ultimately, forgiveness is not an emotion. It is an act of your will – an act of faith."

It helps to remember that God loves the world. He sees us all and knows your heart, as well as the heart of that person you're trying to forgive. He gave His only Son to save you and to save them. If we can see them through God's eyes, as a sinner in need of a Savior, it should motivate us to forgive and do good to them. God is not wanting anyone to eternally perish (Matthew 18:14). His purposes may be fulfilled by your demonstration of His forgiveness.

Pray for the person who hurt or offended you. Pray for their salvation if appropriate, that God would remove the blinders from their eyes. If they are already a believer, ask that God would do His work to free them from bondage to sin and that they would grow in righteousness. It's very hard to pray for and resent someone at the same time. Somehow prayer softens our viewpoint, helps us to see someone as Christ sees them. He is doing His work.

So make the choice to obey Jesus and forgive others. Tell the Lord you're doing this thing, with His power, and ask for His help. Pray for yourself and the person you are forgiving. And ask for more of God's Spirit and power. And then keep asking.

When To Confront

Conflict is an inevitable part of life, and it's hard to know what to do when the conflict happens with someone close to you. Many times the answer is to cover the offense over with love (1 Peter 4:8). But if it's someone you interact with regularly, it may be necessary to talk about your disagreement to clear the air or rectify an ongoing situation.

Review pp. 148-149 in *Bitter Truth*.

25. What should be our main goal when confronting someone?

Pastor Chris Brauns has written *Unpacking Forgiveness: Biblical Answers For Complex Questions and Deep Wounds*. Below you will find his guidelines on when to confront someone which I think are very helpful in this situation.

When you have been offended and are considering confronting someone, ask yourself these questions:

1. *Have I Examined Myself Yet?*
    Review Matthew 7:3-5 about the speck in my brother's eye and the log in my own. We must prayerfully examine our own lives, and ask the Lord to show us our motives.

2. *How Sure Am I That I Am Right?*

In those instances where right and wrong are not clear-cut, it's best to drop the matter. Two observations are in order. First, if there truly is sin in the other person's life, chances are good that this issue will come up again, and you can choose to discuss it at that time. Second, if you always think you are right, you may have a pride problem!

3. *How Important Is This?*

If the source of your conflict is not that important in the long run or the big scope, drop the matter. Don't start a quarrel over it. I made the point above that if you think you are always right, you have a pride problem. Similarly, if you think that *everything* is important, you may have a *sensitivity* problem.

4. *Does This Person Show a Pattern of This Kind Of Behavior?*

If this is a one-time occurrence, wisdom may dictate that you just let the matter drop. Cover it over with love (1 Peter 4:8).

5. *What Do Wise People Counsel Me To Do?*

If appropriate, seek wise counsel. But be careful not to use this as an excuse to gossip. Jesus taught that the second time we confront someone we should take one or two others along. I believe he may have given us that instruction because they could counsel us to drop the matter. They bring a different perspective to the situation.

6. *What Else is Going On In The Other Person's World?*

If this person has been under a great deal of pressure for one reason or another, maybe you should choose to drop it. Likewise, if *you* have been under a great deal of pressure or find yourself very fatigued, you should take into account the possibility that you may be more sensitive than normal. Proverbs 19:11 says "Good sense makes one slow to anger, and it is his glory to overlook an offense." (Brauns, Crossway Books, 2009, pp. 98-102)

26. Read Matthew 18:15-17, where Jesus gives instructions for how to handle it when your brother or sister sins against you. Based on this passage and the above guidelines, describe a situation where it truly would be appropriate to confront someone:

How To Know If You Have Truly Forgiven

Read *Bitter Truth*, pp. 161-163. List the 5 indicators of true forgiveness.

27. Number 1 (p. 161):

It is *possible* that you were not at fault and didn't contribute to the harmful situation at all. This is especially true with children who were victims of abuse or crime. But in most cases of conflict between adults, there is at least *some* poor behavior on both sides. When the Spirit opens your eyes to see how you have contributed to the conflict, it's a sign of His working to help you truly forgive.

28. Number 2:

I hope you can see the difference between remembering and **remembering**. Painful recollections can be harsh and vivid and still cause pain as you recall each hurtful word or action. Other memories are distant and not terribly clear. You remember the situation, but not in great detail. This is the kind of memory we want for the offenses we have forgiven.

29. Number 3 (p. 162):

Again, in the case of children who were harmed, it's not a good idea to pursue a relationship. If the situation is unsafe, you obviously must not put yourself in danger. In some situations, you may have forgiven but the other person has not. As far as it depends on you (Romans 12:18) be peaceable toward them and willing to reconcile.

30. Number 4 (p. 163):

We're told to pray for our enemies and bless them (Matthew 5:44, Romans 12:14). This is truly the hallmark of the Holy Spirit in our lives and proof of His work in helping us forgive.

31. Number 5:

32. What does Luke 6:45 tell us?

The words we speak will prove the state of our hearts.

Application Questions:

A. What is hardest for me in forgiving someone?
B. Is there someone I thought I had forgiven but perhaps really hadn't?
C. Am I more apt to confront others or cover over the offense?

I've discovered that when I'm unforgiving... suddenly everything is wrong with me, God, and the world. Unforgiveness is a poison I choose and it affects everything in my life, not just the isolated instances where I'm angry. ~ Sister Maria Catherine Toon, "Encounters with God's Mercy in Confession and Pilgrimage," www.theimaginativeconservative.org

Lesson 8: Jesus our Healer

Other people are going to find healing in your wounds. Your greatest life messages and your most effective ministry will come out of your deepest hurts. ~ Rick Warren, from *The Purpose Driven Life*

Do You Need To Be Healed?

If you have struggled with any kind of habitual sin (including anger and bitterness), chances are good that you have suffered significant wounds. Many of these wounds contribute to sinful behaviors and leave lasting damage. Sometimes our wounds result from the sinful choices we have made and our shame is added to those consequences.

Here are some common traits of wounded people.
- You often wound others.
- You avoid certain people or places.
- You have made silent inner vows ("I won't let anyone hurt me again," etc.).
- You engage in addictive behaviors.
- You experience ongoing, unresolved grief.
- You suffer from emotional triggers.
- Your thoughts bully you. You feel unworthy, unloved, useless, or disqualified.
- You struggle to verbalize your hurt.

If this describes you, you're right where the enemy wants you. He only has a couple of tactics, and they involve deceiving us and hurling accusations. He wants you to believe lies about yourself and about God. He wants you to believe there's no hope, no healing, and no forgiveness for you. He tells you that you don't deserve another chance because you have blown it so many times. He keeps reminding you of your sin, others' sins against you, and accusing you so the shame stays fresh in your mind and paralyzes you.

1. Read 2 Peter 1:4-8.

2. Peter (the disciple who once blatantly denied knowing Christ) exhorts us to participate in the divine nature and to escape:

3. List the qualities he describes as part of the divine nature.

4. According to 2 Peter 1:8, what will these qualities keep you from being?

5. List the opposites of these (qualities of the divine nature).

Therefore, these are the qualities that will leave you stuck in corruption, hopelessness, and ineffectiveness.

6. 2 Peter 1:3 promises that we have what?

> *The enemy wins when he gets us to torture ourselves by overindulging, neglecting our needs, comparing ourselves with others, dwelling on painful memories, or imagining future painful scenarios. All of these end in "self" and keep us from the One who came to give us abundant life.* ~ Linda Barrick, from Beauty Marks: Healing Your Wounded Heart

The voice of sin may be loud, but the voice of forgiveness is louder. ~ Dwight L. Moody

Jesus Wants To Heal You

When you read the gospels, you can't help but notice all of the healing Jesus did in His earthly ministry. He healed every kind of physical infirmity and also cast out demons from the possessed. There was no kind of healing that He did not undertake: physical, emotional, mental, or spiritual.

Isaiah 61:1-4 is the prophecy of the Messiah's mission, and in Luke 4, Jesus reads these words and tells the crowd, "Today this Scripture is fulfilled in your hearing" (Luke 4:21). We could paraphrase His statement as, "I'm here now, and this is what I'm here to do."

7. Review Isaiah 61:1-4 and describe Jesus' earthly assignment. How many of these are related to healing and restoration?

8. Jesus is Jehovah Rapha, the Almighty Healer. Describe the promises of healing in the following verses:

Psalm 30:2:

Psalm 34:18:

Psalm 103:2-4:

Psalm 107:17-20:

Jeremiah 17:14:

Jeremiah 30:17:

Romans 5:5:

Romans 10:11:

1 Peter 2:24:

Jesus came to earth to bring us hope and healing. Hope is the message of the good news—that God would be reconciled with man because of Jesus' sacrifice on the cross. When we abide in Him, we receive healing of our wounds, release from our bondage. I have experienced this in a life-changing way and greatly desire this for you, too. He is our only hope for healing and true wholeness.

Four Obstacles To Our Healing: Denial, Shame, Unbelief, Unrepentant Sin

#1 Denial —not acknowledging or opening up the wound. When we insist that we are fine and don't need help, we are retreating into isolation and self-protectiveness. Perhaps we've been hurt before when we opened up to someone and aren't willing to take the risk again. We may also be lying to ourselves about just how much of a mess we are. Sometimes it takes the gentle but firm words of a friend to open our eyes so we may see how much we are wounding others or hurting ourselves.

9. Read James 5:16, 19-20. What instructions are given for confessing to one another and asking for help? What promise is given?

10. What warning and exhortations do we receive in Hebrews 3:12-13 about helping our brothers and sisters?

#2 Shame — Shame grows best in isolation. When we keep things hidden and covered up, our shame increases. As we push people away, we nurture further hurt and more shame. Shame differs from guilt because guilt says, "I did bad," while shame says, "I *am* bad." It is the all-encompassing sense that we are inadequate, worthless, and damaged. Shame pervades people's identities creating a sense of unworthiness and rejection.

When I was mired in bitterness, I thought people would be shocked and appalled if they knew what was going on inside my mind and heart. I knew it was sin. I felt shame, but didn't know what to do about it. I was afraid to confess and ask for help, especially from the church leaders. After all, I was on staff at the church and anticipated how disappointed they would be. They might even fire me! But finally, I was desperate enough to ask the elders to pray. Those moments were pivotal and so important in my journey of repentance and healing. I received only kindness and encouragement, not condemnation. Nobody was shocked, and I was deeply moved by the tender prayers they prayed over me. Believe me when I tell you that your pastor, your church leaders, or your women's ministry director will not be scandalized by your sin. They have heard many worse things, I guarantee it!

At the very heart of shame is the absence of relationships, the absence of being known, personal isolation. ~ Ed Welch, from Shame Interrupted

11. Read Hebrews 4:13. How much can we really hide from God?

12. What does Psalm 34:5 promise us?

#3 Unbelief — not believing God's promises. Unbelief is not believing that He *can and will* forgive and heal us when we ask, or it's simply not asking.

Jesus encountered much unbelief and skepticism while on earth. He was not afraid of the questions He was asked by His disciples and friends. Even His cousin John the Baptist had doubts. After languishing in prison for over a year, he became discouraged and sent a message to Jesus. Events weren't unfolding the way he had hoped and he asked, "Are you the One we've been waiting for or should we expect someone else?" (Matthew 11:3)

13. Did Jesus seem upset by this obvious lack of belief? How did He respond? (Matthew 11:4-6)

14. What compliment did He pay to John in the same conversation? (Matthew 11:11)

15. What did Jesus say to "doubting Thomas" in John 20:27?

16. Read the verses immediately following. Did Jesus continue to berate Thomas for his unbelief?

17. What encouraging promise do we receive regarding our temptations in 1 Corinthians 10:13? Does this also apply to the temptation to be cynical and unbelieving?

#4 Unrepentant sin — especially unforgiveness (or bitterness) and idolatry. Any sin that we refuse to recognize or turn from is a hindrance to our healing.

Sin is the best news there is, the best news there could be in our predicament. Because with sin, there's a way out. ~ Nancy Leigh DeMoss from Lies Women Believe

18. When did Christ die for us? (See Romans 5:8)

19. How is Jesus described in Hebrews 4:15-16 and what did He do for us?

Fighting Shame

> *Shame controls many people with feelings of worthlessness, inferiority, rejection, weakness, and failure. It causes people to run away and hide rather than to come out into the Light of Jesus Christ. Understanding how Jesus took our shame and guilt through the Cross and rose again to new life is vital to overcoming feelings of shame and guilt, because only in preaching the right Gospel message to ourselves will one ever overcome feelings of shame and guilt. ~ Ed Welch, from Shame Interrupted*

The curse of sin is experienced in our relationships in the form of shame that seeks to hide from God and others and protect itself from all intruders.

20. Review Hebrews 12:2. How did Jesus react to shame? How can we model Him in this?

The Apostle Peter could be the poster child for shame. After boasting to Jesus that he would die for Him, he cowardly denied even knowing Him. He lingered in the courtyard to see what would happen after Jesus was arrested, but each time he was accused of being one of Jesus' followers, he vehemently denied it.

21. Luke 22:60-62 tells us how Peter reacted when the rooster crowed and he realized what he had done. How is it described?

Let's consider the scene after Jesus' resurrection in John 21. Peter, James, and John, the former fishermen, went back to their old profession after Jesus' death. Perhaps they didn't know what else to do and they invited some of the other disciples to go along.

22. How many disciples were fishing together that morning? (John 21:1-3)

23. Who was the first one to recognize Jesus on the shore? (John 21:7)

24. What did Peter do when he heard this? (John 21:7)

John doesn't tell us specifically, but we can assume the disciples greeted Jesus here.

25. What was Jesus' next instruction? (John 21:10)

26. Who jumped immediately to obey? (John 21:11)

27. John tells us in verse 11 that there were 153 fish in the net. Who may have counted them and why would he have taken the time to do that?

Verses 12-14 recount the Risen Savior and King cooking his friends a humble breakfast on the beach. Afterwards, Jesus pulled Peter aside and asked him to profess his love and loyalty three times.

28. How many times did Peter deny knowing Jesus? (John 18:17, 25-27)

Imagine how awkward Peter must have felt when encountering the Lord. He was probably a confused mixture of joy, regret, shame, and hope. If Jesus had not brought up the subject of his denial, it's unlikely that Peter would have.

> So when we are not open (about our wounds), we are hiding or isolating which not only prevents us from healing, but actually continues to layer fresh layers of shame. Take Peter, for example. He felt great shame for denying the Lord. The Lord forced it into the open with the question, "Do you love me?" (John 21:15). Jesus brought up the subject and then made it clear Peter was not rejected, not worthless, not unacceptable. He made it clear Peter was useful, loved, accepted, and worthwhile. If He had not addressed it directly, it would have been easy for Peter to cover over and not be honest about what he had done. He might have put on a happy face and yet be dying inside. Jesus ripped the wound open, and we see the healed Peter later on in his letter. ~ Beth Wahl, Women's Ministry Director

29. What did Peter write about shame in 1 Peter 2:6?

30. What victorious description of believers does he give in 1 Peter 2:9?

About Idolatry

Dear children, keep yourselves from idols. (1 John 5:21)

What is an idol? It is anything more important to you than God, anything that absorbs your heart and imagination more than God, anything you seek to give you what only God can give. If we look to some created thing to give us the meaning, hope, and happiness that only God himself can give, it will eventually fail to deliver and break our hearts. ~ Tim Keller, from Counterfeit Gods

31. In Ezekiel 14:3, what does God say idols do?

God was saying that the human heart takes **good** things, like a successful career, love, material possessions, even family, and turns them into **ultimate** things. Our hearts make them out to be supremely important in our lives, because, we think, they can give us significance, security, and fulfillment.

When a good thing is turned into a supreme thing, its demands override all other values. We think that idols are bad things, but that is not always the case. The greater the good, the more likely we are to expect that it can satisfy our deepest needs and hopes. Anything can serve as a counterfeit god or idol, especially the very best things in life. Anything can be turned into an idol, and everything has been an idol.

32. In Exodus 20:4-5, God commanded the Israelites to do what?

How do we relate to our idols? We love them, trust them, and obey them. We can identify them by looking at our daydreams and nightmares. What do we dream about, wish for, imagine? Or what is our worst fear or the thing we dread most? This may help us identify potential idols in our lives.

Spend a moment thinking about things that could be potential idols in your life. Fill in the blanks with some options and see if they strike you as true.

I can't possibly live without _____.

If I lose _____, or never have _____, I won't survive.

Tim Keller again:

> *A counterfeit god is anything so central and essential to your life that, should you lose it, your life would feel hardly worth living. An idol has such a controlling*

position in your heart that you can spend most of your passion and energy, your emotional and financial resources, on it without a second thought. It can be family and children, or career and making money, or achievement and critical acclaim, or saving face and social standing. It can be a romantic relationship, peer approval, competence and skill, secure and comfortable circumstances, your beauty or your brains, a great political or social cause, your morality and virtue, or even success in the Christian ministry.

33. Read Isaiah 44:9-20. This passage describes the one who makes and worships idols. Verses 9, 18, and 20 give specific character traits of such a person. List them.

34. What happens to those who worship idols, according to Jeremiah 2:5?

35. What do idols become to those who worship them? (Psalm 106:36)

36. Can you think of examples of how this might happen?

37. What is God's reaction to idol worship in Psalm 78:58-59?

38. How does He express His feelings in Isaiah 42:8? What is idol worship taking away from God?

39. In the New Testament, we are also warned against idols. Read 2 Corinthians 6:16-17. What is the exhortation here?

40. What specific idol is listed at the end of Colossians 3:5?

41. This tempting idol is also listed in 1 Timothy 6:10 and Hebrews 13:5. What is the warning and what is the antidote?

42. Read Psalm 48:14. What is the promise to us?

To fight idolatry, it may be helpful to identify those things that tempt us. What situations, possessions, or people do I look to to find my satisfaction and happiness? What stumbling blocks keep me from fully submitting my heart to God?

After reflecting, place them in the blanks here as a prayer of surrender:

Lord, if I never have _____ or experience _____,

I will be content and trust You. I know You will sustain me even if I were to lose

_____.

Read the accounts of Linda's healing and change in *Bitter Truth*, pp. 173-180.

43. What symptoms of obvious unbelief and idolatry stand out to you?

The Path to Healing

Author Linda Barrick talks about the journey of healing she and her family have been on for the past decade in her book, *Beauty Marks: Healing Your Wounded Heart*. She recommends using Jesus' time of greatest wounding—His crucifixion—as a model to follow.

First, He acknowledged His wound and pain by crying out to God. Matthew 27:46 records:

> *About three in the afternoon Jesus cried out in a loud voice, "Eli, Eli, lema sabachthani?" (which means "My God, my God, why have you forsaken me?")*

He did not deny the suffering He was experiencing, both physical and emotional. The pain of being separated from God in those moments was excruciating and He declared it openly. We must admit that we are wounded and express it to God and others.

Someone has said that a wound must be cleansed with our tears before it can finally begin to heal.

She also points out that healing comes from a personal relationship with God. We are not seeking healing just for its own sake, but rather to know The Healer more intimately. We desire healing so we can love and serve Him more faithfully and more effectively. There's a hymn called "My Goal is God Himself" and the lyrics say in part:

> *My goal is God Himself, not joy, nor peace,*
> *Nor even blessing, but Himself, my God;*
> *'Tis His to lead me there—not mine, but His—*
> *At any cost, dear Lord, by any road.*

If we substitute the word "blessing" here with "healing," we will have the right approach. My goal is God Himself, not just the healing He gives.

Secondly, while Jesus was in the process of being crucified, He was forgiving His tormentors.

44. Record His words in Luke 23:34:

This did not occur after He had risen from the dead and was comfortably reminiscing with His disciples. This was right smack in the middle of the worst torture. What an example of obedience during suffering! The model for us to follow is to obey and forgive, even while still wounded and hurting.

Another point to remember is that Jesus did ask for help. In John 19:28, He declared, "I am thirsty." The Almighty God Incarnate who created water itself asked for a drink. We must take heed of this lesson and not be afraid to ask for others' help when we need it. We are in community, the body of believers, for a reason.

And finally, Barrick points out that Jesus was thinking of others and serving them, even during that horrible day of His crucifixion. He was not focusing on Himself and His own pain, but seeking to minister to those around Him. If you've ever suffered great pain, you know how hard it is to reach outside of your own experience and focus on others. But this is exactly what Jesus did in the midst of unimaginable suffering.

45. Record what He said in Luke 23:28. Who was He concerned for?

46. Who was He ministering to in Luke 23:43?

47. Who was He taking care of in John 19:26?

Barrick writes:

> *While Jesus was wounded, He was helping and serving others. Jesus was showing compassion and caring for his mother instead of focusing on himself. When you're suffering, look to the needs of others. He modeled what I've discovered to be true in my own experience: sometimes the only way to survive or make sense of your own pain is to help someone else. When you're helping, you're healing. Scientific studies support this - serving is directly proportional to healing. One study found that seniors who spent at least 100 hours volunteering each year had 30 percent fewer physical limitations than those who did not volunteer. The more you serve others, the less pain you'll feel, and your heart will begin to heal over time.*

Just before Jesus died, He declared, "Father, into Your hands I commit my spirit." (Luke 23:46) Again, here is an example for us to follow in our times of wounding. We must trust God and His good purposes for us. He is a good Father and can redeem even the worst circumstances.

From our perspective in time looking back, the death of Jesus on the cross is the greatest event in all of history because He provided forgiveness and redemption for us. We would have no hope without it. But from the perspective of those standing around the cross that day, it was the worst imaginable outcome. Their hearts were pierced with grief as they watched the one they loved—and believed to be the Messiah—suffer and die. We must get into the habit of saying, "Father, into Your hands I commit my spirit" when things look difficult and bleak.

Steps to Healing

1. Acknowledge your wounds. Do not deny the pain you feel, but express it to God and to others. Don't be afraid to ask for help from church leaders or Christian counselors if necessary. Ask others to pray for you. Denying that we have wounds will only make them fester and cause more problems.

2. Draw near to God. "The Lord is near to all who call on him, to all who call on him in truth." (Psalm 145:18) God wants our love, our hearts, and our worship. We can be honest about how we're feeling and what we're struggling with. He promises to help us.

James 4:8-10 says: *Come near to God and he will come near to you. Wash your hands, you sinners, and purify your hearts, you double-minded. Grieve, mourn and wail. Change your laughter to mourning and your joy to gloom. Humble yourselves before the Lord, and he will lift you up.*

We must desire an intimate relationship with the Healer even more than we desire our own healing. Healing for its own sake is not the objective; loving and serving Jesus better through health and wholeness is our goal.

3. Ask in faith to be healed. Believe that you are forgiven. Refuse to wallow in the shame. In John 21, when Peter met Jesus on the beach, we saw how Jesus restored Peter and commissioned him to lead the church, despite his failings. We know Peter believed he was forgiven because of how he acted afterwards. He became the leader of the Jerusalem church and wrote the victorious epistles of 1 and 2 Peter. According to church history, he died as a martyr by being crucified upside down.

4. Obey. Examine yourself and confess sin if necessary, but develop the habit of quick forgiveness. Fight bitterness and idolatry in your life. Determine to obey Jesus and live righteously no matter what.

> Barrick says: *Forgiveness itself doesn't heal our wounds; only God can do that. Forgiveness sets us free from the bitterness that infects our wounds and positions us so that God can make us whole. In that sense, forgiveness is necessary for our healing to continue.*

The story of the Ten Lepers in Luke 17 illustrates the importance of belief and obedience. They approached Jesus and asked Him to have pity and heal them. He immediately got to the point in verse 14 and said, "Go, show yourselves to the priests." He took pity on them as they had asked. He could probably see (and smell) that they were in dire straits. This is the same compassionate Savior who sees you and knows what you need. Surprisingly, the ten lepers set off for town right away at Jesus' instructions.

This shows that they believed Him, although they were not yet healed. I know if I were one of them, I would have shot up my hand and said "Excuse me? Jesus? We can't go into town or to the temple because, you know, we're lepers! We're outcasts! You need to heal us first!" But this isn't what they did. They had faith and obeyed. And the next line (Luke 17:14b) says:

AND AS THEY WENT, THEY WERE CLEANSED.

Because they believed Jesus could heal, and because of their faith, they obeyed Him. They didn't question or clarify or doubt, they simply acted. And while they were being obedient and doing what He told them to, they were healed.

5. Serve others. Proverbs 11:25 says "Whoever refreshes others will be refreshed." Philippians 2:3-4 admonishes us not to think selfishly, but to put others' interests above our own. Looking outside ourselves, especially when we are hurting, gives us a new

perspective and furthers our healing. A life of service to others benefits us physically, emotionally, and spiritually. It's modeling Jesus and His behavior.

6. Look for eternal purpose in your wound. Instead of asking *why*, ask *how*? How can God redeem this in my life? How can He make me more like Jesus through this? Is there a way I can minister to others because I am uniquely qualified by my suffering?

We know that His ways are far above our ways and His thoughts far above ours (Isaiah 55:8-9). We may see in our lifetime why He allowed some of our hurts, or we may never understand His purposes until we see Him face to face. Either way, we can trust Him to be good and always do what is right (1 John 2:29).

My Story of Healing

As I tell others about my journey from bitterness to repentance, I will often say, "I've been healed."

What do I mean by that? I mean that the wounds that used to be so ever-present and painful are gone. When I think about the lack of love and affection in my childhood, the awkwardness and rejection of my teen years, I no longer feel that hurt. When I reflect on my young adult years and the many mistakes I made in friendships and marriage, I don't experience that sharp regret. The shame is gone. I can admit to the lies I believed and how I was deceived. The years of struggle with my dear boss/pastor are great examples of what *not to* do, and I freely share my failures with the hope of encouraging others.

How did this happen? It was a process. I hardly knew what was happening, it occurred so gradually.

A few years ago I spoke to a group of ladies from my home church. I told all my sad stories, details about how nasty and awful I was to my boss, my husband, my parents. I recounted the mean things I said and thought and did. I told that group that they, too, could have freedom from the bondage of bitterness. I said that on the other side was healing and joy!

Afterwards, one lady came up to me and kindly said, "You were brave to share all that detail, to be so vulnerable. That must have been hard for you." I pondered that and replied, "No, it really wasn't." And I realized in that moment the extent of the healing that has taken place in my heart. *While I was on the way*, I was healed, like the ten lepers in Luke 17:14. While I was learning about repentance and forgiveness and putting them into practice day after day, God healed many of my hurts.

I praised God as I thought of myself years ago and how I wanted desperately to conceal the fact that I was a mess. And now it's almost the opposite: I am eager to share with you my many failures in order to greater showcase God's power to change a bitter wretch like me! I also feel a burden for women who struggle as I did, who need to be warned and encouraged.

That's what I mean when I refer to "being healed." Jesus wants to heal you, too! Ask Him, and then obey as the Holy Spirit works in your heart and mind.

Application Questions:

A. Do you see any of the symptoms of a wounded person in yourself?
B. Can you identify the obstacle or obstacles that prevent your healing?
C. Have you asked Jesus to forgive and heal you?

My favorite characteristic of God is that He is redemptive. Nothing is lost or wasted with God; no circumstance is hopeless in the kind hands of the Master Teacher. ~ Dr. Rob Reimer

Lesson 9: Developing the Transformed Mind

Sow a thought and you reap an action; sow an act and you reap a habit; sow a habit and you reap a character; sow a character and you reap a destiny. ~ Ralph Waldo Emerson

Previously in Lesson 6, we discussed the steps to overcoming bitterness (or any other debilitating sin, for that matter). The last step was to let your mind be transformed by God the Holy Spirit. In my opinion, this is the most critical element of this process, the one that takes the longest, and the one that produces the greatest healing. Changing our minds is essential, and it changes our outlook, our attitudes, and our entire lives!

The term "transformed mind" comes from Romans 12:2.

1. Write this verse out, using several different translations. The word "conform" here is from the Greek word *syschematizo*. It means to be *patterned after or molded by*. Notice the differences in how it's phrased, especially in the NLT.

2. According to this verse, what is one benefit we receive from this mindset?

Author Lysa TerKeurst, in her book *Uninvited,* says,

> According to Romans 12:2, the only way to know God's best for you is not to let your thinking be conformed to the patterns of the world but to be transformed by the renewing of your mind. That renewing is not a brief spiritual inspiration that comes from brushing up against the truth. It is anakainosis, which is a change of heart and life. A heart softened by God's truth. And a life transformed by the application of God's truth.

3. What other benefits of the transformed mind are listed in the following verses?

Philippians 4:7:

Romans 8:6:

Isaiah 26:3:

Isaiah 40:31:

Read *Bitter Truth*, pp. 117-124 about fighting the war in the battlefield of the mind.

4. List the suggestions for fighting this battle (all in italics).

5. After pondering these, describe which may be most difficult for you and why.

We will summarize these into four main points and then explore further. In developing the transformed mind, we must :

       A. Remember we're in a spiritual battle
       B. Control what we allow into our minds
       C. Fight our natural tendencies to selfishness
       D. Develop the habit of thanksgiving

A. Remember that we're at war and up against a powerful enemy.

We must constantly be on our guard and stay vigilant about what's going on in our minds. *Think about what you're thinking about.* The enemy wants us trapped in selfish or self-destructive thoughts, remembering old lies, and following the world's beliefs and philosophies. His desire is to keep us focused on problems, worries, and what-ifs.

6. According to Ephesians 6:11-12, what and where is the cosmic battle?

7. Where does your mind automatically go whenever you are stressed or upset?

8. If *you* were your enemy, what thoughts would you attempt to plant in your mind?

9. Read 1 Peter 5:8. We are warned to be alert and _____ . Why?

10. What is the Apostle Paul worried about in 2 Corinthians 11:3?

The battle for righteousness always begins in our thought lives. Our minds are true battlefields. We must be aware and not let our guard down. God has given us weapons to fight with, and we can be victorious. Fight the tendency to ignore the battle, to go on autopilot, or to "mind-drift."

Pastor Rob Reimer speaks of this temptation:

> I struggle with what I call "mind drift" - the natural tendency of my mind to drift to my greatest pressing problem. It isn't conscious. I'm not intentionally thinking about this problem. But as the day goes on, I'll find my mind keeps drifting back to that problem. The law of entropy states that a field, if it is not tended, will move toward chaos. It doesn't naturally drift toward a well-kept, fruitful vineyard; that requires hard work. It is the same with my soul. My mind naturally drifts toward my greatest problems. If I have a problem-centered perspective in life, I'll have problem-centered living. If I have a victorious perspective, I'll have victorious living. The battle is to fix my eyes on Jesus, the ultimate victor, and keep my eyes there. We have to practice the presence of Jesus and not the presence of our problems.

Science writer, David DiSalvo, in his book *What Makes Your Brain Happy And Why You Should Do the Opposite*, says:

> Some studies find that most of us are mentally elsewhere between 30-50% of our waking hours. Daydreaming - wandering off mentally - serves a purpose. Being in default increases with stress, boredom, chaos and fatigue. It is also linked to creativity. Our brains are happy to go there, and we can sometimes ruminate on problems and develop solutions while drifting.

DiSalvo then goes on to explain that *excessive* mental wandering often leads to persistent negative thoughts and subsequent depression. Our brains want to and like to drift off because it is the path of least resistance, but it isn't what's healthiest for us.

Weapons We Can Fight With

11. What tools are at our disposal to fight with in the battlefield of our minds? Answer from the following verses.

Colossians 3:16:

1 John 5:4:

John 8:31-32:

2 Corinthians 10:4:

Ephesians 6:17:

2 Timothy 1:7:

The weapons we fight with are not the weapons of the world. On the contrary, they have divine power to demolish strongholds. We demolish arguments and every pretension that sets itself up against the knowledge of God, and we take captive every thought to make it obedient to Christ. (2 Corinthians 10:4-5 NIV)

In the NIV, we are told to demolish arguments and every pretension that sets itself up against the knowledge of God.

12. Look up 2 Corinthians 10:4-5 in a few other translations. What other words are used in place of *arguments* and *pretensions?*

Synonyms for pretension include *disguise, hypocrisy, charade, fake, lie, show-off, and phony.*

13. What kinds of arguments would go up against the knowledge of God? List some examples.

14. What statements of hypocrisy, charade, or pretension would go against the knowledge of God?

15. Have you battled agains any of these?

16. We take every thought captive to obey Christ (2 Corinthians 10:5). What does this mean and how can we do it practically?

So many of us, even Christians, complain about our struggle against sin, but then we secretly supply Satan with all the ammunition he needs. We know we shouldn't be reading that book. We know the telephone conversation we had yesterday was less than glorifying to the Lord. We know the unforgiveness we've harbored for so long is hardening into rage. But still we cling to it—and then we wonder why we have such a hard time making positive changes in our lives. We must be willing to take an active role in the battle. ~ Joanna Weaver, Having a Mary Heart in a Martha World

B. GIGO - Garbage In, Garbage Out.

This is an old computer acronym meaning whatever you program into your computer (or brain) is what you will get out of it. We must analyze what we are thinking and take steps to control the content.

17. What does the Bible specifically tell us to think about?

Matthew 22:37:

Romans 8:5:

Philippians 4:8:

Colossians 3:2:

1 Peter 1:13:

2 Peter 3:1:

Psalm 119:11:

We must pattern our thinking to be like Christ's and not be pushed into the world's mold. The enemy wants us to be conformed to the world's thinking and to think just like they do. How can we know the difference? We must be diligent in our study of God's Word and know it well. I have heard that government agents who investigate counterfeiting study authentic currency in great detail. In order to identify a fake, they must know for sure what the real thing looks like!

18. Think about and discuss some of the worldviews prevalent today that are in direct contrast to the teachings of the Bible.

19. What are we told *not* to dwell on?

Matthew 6:25-34:

Mark 13:11:

Luke 12:25-26:

Philippians 3:19:

Romans 13:14:

John 14:27:

Am I Believing Truth or Lies?

Just as a reminder, who is the first and biggest liar?

Do we want to believe what he says or what God says?

1 Corinthians 2:16 tells us that *we have the mind of Christ.*

20. What are the characteristics of God's mind versus man's? (Numbers 23:19)

Identifying Lies We May Believe

21. Read *Bitter Truth*, pp. 36-40 and list the 5 beliefs or lies I once believed.

–

–

–

–

–

Do any of these sound familiar? Are you tempted to any of these yourself? Here's a list of some commonly-believed lies:

- I am worthless unless I perform.
- I am not as good as others.
- I am permanently unacceptable, not worthy of saving.
- God can't use me because of some sin I have committed.
- I ought to be more than I am.
- I deserve more than God gave me.
- Life should be fair.
- God speaks to other people but not me.
- He wants other people to know His love but not me.
- He answers other people's prayers but not mine.
- God won't meet my needs. I need to take matters into my own hands.

Lies only have power when you believe them and act accordingly.

If a friend tells you that it's sunny and 70 degrees outside (in January), and advises you to wear shorts and flip-flops, you may not believe him. However, if you do believe him and dress as he advises, you will find yourself in great discomfort and possibly danger when you discover that it's actually 20 degrees outside and snowing!

The lie affects you only if you act upon it.

Some lies may take the form of expectations. We must recognize when we are making judgement calls about the way things *should be*, in our opinion. We might tell ourselves, "I should be happy, or I deserve to have _____." This is the influence of the world's thinking and philosophy.

We all have desires and longings. The problem emerges when our desires change into demands and our longings become expectations. Our culture encourages people to demand their rights and feel entitled to certain treatment. But this is a lie: none of us deserve anything more than God's wrath. We are all sinners and aren't entitled to anything except judgment.

Jesus promised us abundant life in John 10:10, but that didn't necessarily mean comfort and ease. It meant joy, peace, and a meaningful purpose beyond ourselves as we become intimately connected with Him and participate in His kingdom work.

22. Connect the lie that the world uses to influence us with the opposite truth of God's Word: (use arrows)

God accepts me: I'm not so bad and I'm trying.	James 5:12
Following Christ will make life boring.	Romans 3:10-12
Sexual behavior is based on preferences.	Philippians 2:3-4
I deserve to be happy.	2 Timothy 3:16-17
We are all basically good.	John 10:10
Live and let live.	Hebrews 13:4
I need to look out for myself.	Romans 2:5
If you hurt me, I should hurt you back.	Jeremiah 17:10
The Bible is not an absolute authority.	James 5:19-20
It doesn't matter if I don't keep my commitments.	Matthew 5:44

The truth can transform you as much as a lie can destroy you. ~ Tricia Bates, Women's Ministry Director

Compiling a List of Truth (God's Promises)

We can fight the lies of the enemy by believing truth. We must know God's Word thoroughly and what He has promised us. If the lie you are tempted to believe is about a certain person, ask God to help you construct positive, merciful messages about them. If the lie is regarding a situation you experienced, ask the Lord to show you how it can be redeemed or how you can help others because of it.

Read pp. 119-120 in *Bitter Truth*, "A page from my story."
23. How did I change my thinking about that awful meeting?

24. What is a conflict or painful situation where changing your thinking would help?

25. Review pp. 120-122 in *Bitter Truth* and list some of God's promises that we can cling to.

So what is true today? Right now? Here are some more assurances from our Heavenly Father of His love and care for us.

26. Find the comfort and promise in each passage.

James 5:11:

Psalm 143:8:

Lamentations 3:22-24:

2 Corinthians 12:9-11:

Zephaniah 3:17:

Truth Vs. Our Emotions

Feelings are, with a few exceptions, good servants. But they are disastrous masters. ~ Dallas Willard

Your emotions are not always reliable indicators of reality. Don't let them boss or bully you! Let them be a guide to indicate where the battle within you is raging so you can attack it with the proper promises of truth. As we discussed in the Forgiveness lesson, your emotions may not always immediately catch up to your decisions. Sometimes we need to just grit our teeth and choose to believe truth, even if it doesn't always *feel* true at the moment. Our feelings follow the direction our thoughts take us in.

In *Don't Follow Your Heart,* Jon Bloom says,

> *God designed our emotions to be gauges - meant to report to you, not rule you. The pattern of your emotions will give you a reading on what your hope is, because they are wired into what you believe and value - and how much. Emotions reveal what your heart loves, trust, fears.*

Here are some thoughts from Christian counselor and author, Leslie Vernick, instructing us how to break free from our negative emotions, in her book, *Lord, I Just Want to Be Happy*:

> *…it's important that we not allow our emotions or even our thoughts to define who we are…. When you say I'm angry instead of I'm aware I'm feeling angry, you're*

likely to get stuck in your anger…. Creating this little bit of space empowers us to become aware of a larger self that can help the other part of us that is caught in the negative spin of emotional pain.

Pain usually has a reason. It is often trying to tell us something so we will take action.

Here are some additional questions that will help you figure out what your feelings are trying to tell you. Is there a problem I'm not facing? What purpose do my negative emotions serve right now?

… we have learned that much of our unhappiness results from wrong thinking and wrong habits, not always situational factors.

What our mind habitually dwells on will affect us emotionally and physically. When you think negative thoughts you will feel negative…. We are to take every thought captive to the obedience of Christ (2 Corinthians 10:5)…. we're to examine every thought, whether positive or negative, through the lens of Scripture to evaluate whether or not we are telling ourselves the truth.

I have to admit, the past few days as I've been writing this section, I have been struggling with my emotions. Nothing drastic, just a pervading feeling of sadness or the "blues." I know it's not a coincidence *(Hello? It's a war!)*, so I'm trying to pinpoint what subtle lies I'm hearing or believing to produce these feelings. The messages are familiar, the words *worthless, annoying, and ridiculous* often roll around in my head. And I know they are not true! I know it, but it's still a battle to fight well. I'm taking these thoughts captive, remembering what is true, looking for things to be thankful for.

Lord, thank you for the abundant blessings of today. Help me to keep my mind fixed on You and Your promises! Thank you for Your unfailing love for me. Please help me to do what You've called me to do and not fall into a pit of negative thinking or succumb to my emotions. Thank you for the victory I can have through You.

I want you to know that I get it. It's often tough to fight against our emotions and negative thoughts. If it were easy, it wouldn't be called a battle!

Go back to Lesson 5 and review our identity in Christ. Remember ABC—ARF ?

27. What is the promise in Psalm 36:9?

Strong emotions especially can create significant blind spots. When we are furiously angry, in love, or in the grip of cravings and addictions, we may not see things clearly. Often it is our family or close friends who see things we don't and can warn us of dangers ahead. We must rely on the advice and perspective of those we love and trust.

Proverbs 19:20 tells us: "Listen to advice and accept instruction, that you may gain wisdom in the future."

> *Feelings, in and of themselves, are not wrong. How we feel is just how we feel. In fact, God created our emotions and is emotional Himself. For example, He feels joy (Luke 10:21), anger (Matthew 21:12-17), grief and sorrow (John 11:33-35) and sadness (Mark 14:34). We will experience hurt, fear and anger. However, they must be managed or they can run wild, tempting us to believe things that aren't true. My life is hopeless. Nothing will ever change. I'm stupid and unimportant. No one cares about me. I always flub it, so why even try? When we believe such lies, we may decide never to trust anyone again, seek revenge, or sink into bitterness. Or we may become angry and withdraw from God or turn to various addictions to dull the pain. ~ Becky Harling, from Rewriting Your Emotional Script*

You can't always help how you feel, but you can choose and control how you will think. And how you think, consistently and with time, will change the way you feel.

C. Fight selfishness and self-centered thinking.

Let's be honest—most of our thoughts revolve around ourselves. After all, we spend many hours taking care of our bodies. We must feed them, wash them, dress them, and ensure proper rest. We protect ourselves when an object comes flying toward us. If we're too cold, we put on more clothing. We think about how to make ourselves happy, and we rebel when a situation is not comfortable. We are naturally self-centered, but this is not how God desires us to live.

28. When we are in Christ, what change occurs? (Ephesians 4:22-24)

29. What should our new attitude be, according to Romans 15:5?

30. Read Philippians 2:3-4. What are we told *not to* do?

31. How can we follow Christ's mindset from Philippians 2:5-8?

Self-Indulgence and Self-Pity

More thoughts from Vernick:

> … it does feel good to indulge, even if only temporarily. That's why we do it… The problem is, the feeling doesn't last… What started as pleasure eventually becomes bondage (2 Peter 2:19).
>
> Self-pity is a toxic form of self-indulgence we don't always realize it as destructive.
>
> Our self-pitying thoughts often revolve around our abilities, attributes, and assets, or the lack of these things, as well as what other people have done to us.
>
> The only one that can stop your pity party is you.

32. Why do we indulge in self-pity?

33. What does 2 Peter 2:19 say about indulging ourselves?

Read pp. 129-136 in *Bitter Truth* about hurt feelings, selfishness, and self-pity.

34. What sin did Doug commit against me? What contributed to my bitterness?

35. What does James 3:14-16 say about selfish ambition? What are the results?

36. Can you think of an instance where your feelings were hurt and it evolved into self-pity?

No sin is worse than the sin of self-pity,
because it removes God from the throne of our lives,
replacing Him with our own self-interests.
It causes us to open our mouths only to complain,
and we simply become spiritual sponges -
always absorbing, never giving, and never being satisfied.
And there is nothing lovely or generous about our lives.
~ Oswald Chambers

Self-Hatred

37. Look up 2 Corinthians 7:8-11. Describe the difference between godly sorrow and worldly sorrow. What does godly sorrow produce?

One of the messages the world tells us is, "Good self-esteem is important. You must love and accept yourself." Instead, Scripture tells us that we are wicked, sinful, and without hope of change. Yet despite this, we are accepted by the Father because of Christ's sacrifice on our behalf. We are unendingly and unconditionally loved. We are the precious sons and daughters of the King of the universe!

In *When People Are Big and God Is Small,* Ed Welch says,

Low self-esteem usually means that I think too highly of myself. I'm too self-involved, I feel I deserve better than what I have. The reason I feel bad about myself is that I aspire to something more. I want just a few minutes of greatness.

My self-esteem must be rightly based on who *God says* I am, not on any inherent goodness or righteousness I possess. Left to our own devices, we would all live as God's enemies and blatantly self-destruct.

Vernick continues:

> *Please don't mistake self-hatred for godly sorrow or biblical repentance. (See Paul's teaching on the difference in 2 Corinthians 7:8-13.) Self-hatred doesn't lead us toward Christ; rather it turns us in on ourselves. It erodes our soul and spirit like acid on metal.*

> *Self-hatred is nothing more than wounded pride. We are disappointed that we are not more than we are. The truth is, we're not—and when we can accept that truth, we will have incredible freedom and peacefulness. Why? Because we know and rest in the good news that Jesus loves and accepts us in spite of who we are or what we have or have not done.*

D. Practice gratitude or thanksgiving.

Self-pity, which we are naturally drawn to, is the polar opposite of thanksgiving. You cannot do both. It's either one or the other! We are either thinking of ourselves as victims or as recipients of blessing. It's impossible to believe both at the same time.

38. What are we commanded to do in 1 Thessalonians 5:18?

39. Read Lamentations 3:18-20. What is the writer remembering here?

40. Continue on with Lamentations 3:21-26. What is he now focusing on in these verses?

Many of the Psalms also follow this pattern: the writer laments his troubles and then turns his mind to God's promises of deliverance. He changes his mind from depressed to thankful. See Psalm 73 as an example. This is a pattern we must recognize and choose when our minds are tempted to focus on only negative things.

41. Look up and list some synonyms for *thankless*: (thesaurus.com is a good resource)

42. Are these adjectives you would want applied to you?

Pastor and author Mark Buchanan speaks of this:

> *Thanklessness becomes its own prison. Persisted in, it becomes its own hell, where there is outer darkness and gnashing of teeth. Thanklessness is the place God doesn't dwell, the place, that, if we inhabit it too often, He turns us over to. "See to it that no one misses the grace of God," Hebrews 12:15 says, "and that no bitter root grows up to cause trouble and defile many." Thanklessness troubles and defiles many, because first it troubles and defiles the one in whom bitterness takes root. ~ from The Holy Wild: Trusting in the Character of God*

We will explore these four main points again in the next lesson, while discussing more about how to practically apply them.

Application Questions:
A. Do you often think about what you're thinking about? Is this difficult?
B. What are some lies the enemy has told you? Do you struggle to *not* believe them?
C. Do you struggle with self-pity, self-indulgence, or self-hatred?
D. Which of these is probably the most challenging to overcome?

If you don't like something, change it. If you can't change it, change the way you think about it. ~ Unknown

Lesson 10: Applying the Transformed Mind

We have to practice the presence of Jesus and not the presence of our problems. ~ Dr. Rob Reimer

We discussed the four main tenets of the transformed mind in Lesson 9, and now it's time to talk about practical ways to apply them and incorporate them into your life.

1. Just as a reminder, list the four characteristics here.

2. What did Jesus say is the greatest commandment in Matthew 22:37?

In Matthew 22:37, Jesus said the first and greatest commandment was: Love the Lord your God with all your heart and with all your soul and with all your mind.

> *If we aren't intentional about our thoughts – how we think about ourselves, other people, life, our circumstances, and God – how can we ever possibly love Him with all of our mind? We can't. Without being mindful of our minds, we will never fully realize the greatest love and calling on our lives… God discerns our every thought. Our thinking matters that much to Him, because He designed us in a way that our thinking is the foundation of how our lives go – at least how we react to things and make decisions. Therefore, being aware of and purposeful about our minds is essential to living the life God desires us to live. ~ Tracy Wainwright, from A Transformed Mind: Change Your Thoughts to Change Your Life*

Habits Are Powerful

Such as are your habitual thoughts, such also will be the character of your mind; for the soul is dyed by the thoughts. ~ Marcus Aurelius

New York Times reporter and author, Charles Duhigg, says in his book, *The Power of Habit:*

> *Habits come from the choices we deliberately made at some point. But with repetition, we start making these choices automatically. Both good and bad behavioral patterns become wired into our brains. Bad habits often form so gradually that we aren't aware of them until they start causing problems. Some habits govern trivial matters, like brushing teeth and tying shoes. But others profoundly influence health, productivity, finances and happiness.*

Duhigg explains that habits are merely feedback loops that we run over and over until a behavior occurs without conscious thought. They are formed via a "habit loop," cue—routine—reward. First, there's the cue that instigates the process. It is the stimulus, the cause, the originating factor. It can be sadness, stress, anxiety, boredom, fear, a certain place, or a relationship. This is the situation that exists that triggers the routine. Next, the routine, is the action that we perform. We eat a donut, smoke a cigarette, snap at the children, check our phones, or snooze in front of the TV. We do this in order to receive the reward: relaxation, satisfaction, elevated blood sugar, or a feeling of accomplishment. The reward can be a pleasurable feeling or the avoidance of something painful.

This habit loop can be as innocent as how we wash in the shower or as destructive as online gambling or pornography. Bad habits are often formed automatically, but good habits can be cultivated with effort.

Four Facts About Habits (from Duhigg's The Power of Habit)

- *Habits save brain effort. Habits free up our prefrontal cortex for complex thoughts while other routines are running on autopilot. This is why we can plan out our day while brushing our teeth or daydream in the shower.*
- *Habits are diverse. A cue to start a habit can be almost anything, routines can be simple or complex, and rewards can vary from physical pleasure to emotions. Even for the same routine, individuals may have very different cues and rewards.*
- *Habits can form both with and without our awareness. They develop whenever a cue-routine-reward sequence occurs repeatedly. We can construct habits deliberately, but they can also form unconsciously. Because habits work with the brain on autopilot, we are often unaware that a habit is forming or driving our behavior.*
- *Habits are persistent. They are encoded in the basal ganglia and persist even when we want to get rid of them.*

3. Give an example of the cue—routine—reward from a habit you regularly perform, however innocent it may be.

Unfortunately our brains can't tell good habits from bad ones. Once a bad habit is formed, it persists, waiting for the right cues to trigger the routine and rewards. Unless you deliberately fight a habit, it will happen automatically. However, by learning to observe cues and rewards, we can replace bad routines with better ones.

To change a habit you must focus on the routine, not the cue or reward. You can't eliminate the cue, nor can you eliminate the desire for the reward. The only part you can change is the routine. Do something else that can give a similar reward when the stimulus hits. Duhigg goes on to explain *"The Golden Rule of Habit Change"* —

Alcoholism is more than a habit; it is also a physical addiction and potentially influenced by genetic factors. But AA doesn't address any of the physiological aspects of alcoholism. Instead, AA uses the Golden Rule of Habit Change to alter the routines of alcoholics.

The first step is finding cues for alcohol use. The steps ask participants to list the reasons, situations and cues that trigger urges to drink. The next step is to identify the rewards of drinking. Surprisingly, feeling intoxicated is usually not the reward being sought. Instead, alcoholics usually drink to escape, relax, seek companionship, reduce anxiety or to feel an emotional release.

Finally, AA provides a new routine - a system of meetings and companionship - to replace the routine of drinking in order to get the same rewards. AA meetings and sponsors aim to provide escape, distraction, companionship and relief in place of drinking. By inserting a new routine, AA has helped 10 million people achieve sobriety.

Four Steps To Change An Unwanted Habit

1. Identify the routine (the behavior that repeats, despite your best efforts).
2. Experiment with rewards (try something else and observe if it satisfies).
3. Isolate the cue (most cues fall into these categories: location, time, emotional state, other people, or immediately preceding action).
4. Plan a new routine: "when (insert cue), I will (insert new routine), to (insert reward)."

Duhigg gives the following example:

> Cue - stress at work
> Routine - watch TV all night
> Reward - mental escape
> **Instead, modify the routine:**
> Cue - stress at work
> Routine - go for a walk, then allow 1 hour of TV viewing
> Reward - mental escape plus the beneficial feeling of exercise

Here are two examples I came up with for how we can apply *The Golden Rule of Habit Change* to our thoughts:

Cue - a meeting at work
Routine - I begin thinking about the reasons I dislike my job
Reward - self-comfort via self-pity
Instead:
Cue - a meeting at work
Routine - taking charge of my thoughts and consciously reminding myself of all the good aspects of my job
Reward - happy and positive feelings (not the same reward, but a more satisfying one)

Cue - phone call from my daughter
Routine - I worry about what kinds of unsafe situations she may be in; I'm concentrating on the "what-if's"
Reward - self-comfort, a sense of satisfaction over doing something
Instead:
Cue- phone call from my daughter
Routine- taking control of my thoughts and choosing to pray for her, leaving her in God's hands
Reward - peace and hope

Duhigg goes on to say: *While The Golden Rule of Habit Change is a powerful tool for reshaping habits, some really stubborn habits are hard to change without one more ingredient: belief. Often in stressful situations, we revert back to our previous bad habits. For a habit to stay changed, individuals must have the conviction that change is possible. On their own, individuals may doubt their ability to change, but support from a group or community can help build conviction.*

4. What's a comforting reminder from Hebrews 2:18?

How long does it take to develop or change a habit? Duhigg says it takes as long as it takes. People are all different and the ingrained habits are at various levels of formation. Some people say it takes 28 days to establish or break a habit, but we are all unique.

Author and science writer David DiSalvo agrees. He says:

Habits change how our brains work. What begins as a behavior morphs into changes in brain circuitry, and with repetition and time those changes strengthen and endure. We can force the routine into conscious mind space and change it. Start with one bad habit you want to change and stick with it until it works. For ingrained habits, you're going to wrestle with unconsciously controlled behaviors for as long as it takes. ~ from Brain Changer: How Harnessing Your Brain's Power To Adapt Can Change Your Life

What Are You *Thinking*?

We usually have one of three different types of thoughts running through our minds. I've broken them into three categories: *Neutral, Negative, and Positive*.

Neutral — This is mindless chatter: the to-do list, observations about things we see, and wishes and daydreams. These are the things that routinely come into our minds during the day. Generally we don't even recall these thoughts, and they are mostly harmless. We discussed the tendency to go into autopilot or mind-drift in Lesson 9, and this can be restful, as long as we don't indulge in it too often or allow it to become a regular escape.

Negative — These thoughts are anything that leads us toward sin. They include lies the enemy wants us to believe. These incorporate comparison, envy, and a critical spirit toward others. We may also indulge in anger, lust, or obsessive thoughts that become idolatry. And then there are the lies we have learned to believe because of past painful experiences. These may sound like, "I'm not good enough. Nobody wants to hear from me. God doesn't listen to my prayers. I can't do this." Sometimes it may be hard to discern which are from the enemy and which originate from our own selfish nature and wounded pasts.

Positive — These things are lovely, true, and encouraging; being thankful, thinking well of others. Thinking about how I may help or encourage those around me. Communing with God, praying, and listening for His voice. Meditating on Scripture or worship song lyrics.

As I have learned to pay attention to what I'm thinking about, I find that many of my thoughts on any given day are either neutral or negative. Positive thoughts often take a conscious effort, and sometimes when I'm busy or tired I just don't want to extend it. It's always easier to take the path of least resistance or shift into mind-drift.

A common acronym for the negative thinking that plagues us is ANTS: Automatic Negative Thoughts. We must stomp out the nasty and annoying ANTS in our thought lives! I love the picture it brings to mind. Ew! Nobody wants a swarm of ants all over their picnic.

But first we must be aware; we must be thinking about what we are thinking about. DiSalvo calls this process *metacognition*:

> *Metacognition is our ability to think about our thinking. Any time we are reflecting upon our thinking process and knowledge, we are metacognizing. It's problem*

solving, detachment, and a way to gain perspective. This is our most powerful internal tool to adjust our thinking and improve thinking outcomes. The more metacognitively aware we are, the less we will use autopilot to guide our thinking processes.

DiSalvo explains that what we repeat to ourselves over time will eventually become the reality we perceive ourselves to be living. If we indulge in *thinking errors* (we could also call them ANTS), it establishes neural patterns in our brains. We find ourselves falling into errors because those 'tracks' are physical structures that have developed in our brains over the years and we are trained to follow them.

Other studies on the brain mention visible "grooves" that can be seen in brain scans. These guide our thinking into familiar "trenches of thought" that have been developed over time. After change has occurred, either counseling to help overcome addictions or a major thinking shift, doctors can actually see the difference in the brain scans. It takes considerable effort to fill in the old grooves and develop new ones, but it is possible with time and effort.

DiSalvo encourages us by saying that change is possible; our personalities are not static. He says, "The leopard and his famous spots were always a misplaced metaphor."

This is the viewpoint of secular scientists. Changing your habits and your thinking is possible, they say. What does Jesus say?

5. Write out Romans 8:5-6 in several different translations. I especially like how it's phrased in the NLT.

Right here is the prescription for change! A Holy Spirit-controlled mind leads to life and peace. A thought life submitted to God produces joy, meaning, and purpose. We let Jesus take charge of our thoughts and order our thought lives according to His instructions. It involves obedience, submission, and trust.

The alternative involves much pain and misery. The Bible calls it death! I well remember those days of anguish, when I engaged in all sorts of "thinking errors" or ANTS. Life was hard and unjust and everyone was against me. No one appreciated me, no one wanted me around, and no one cared about my efforts (or so I thought). I was dealt an unfair hand and things seemed hopeless. This is the mind controlled by the sinful-human-selfish nature! And it's an awful pit to be stuck in.

Test the fruit of your thoughts

When you find yourself thinking about something, ask yourself these questions:

- Is this thought neutral, negative, or positive?
- Does it inspire me to run to God or run *from* Him?
- Does it help me love others or am I tearing them down?
- Am I believing what God says is true about me when I am thinking this?
- Am I believing what God says is true about His church and His kingdom when I am thinking this?

6. While not speaking specifically of our thoughts, what are the principles in Matthew 3:8 and Matthew 7:16?

7. How will we bear fruit in every good work (and thought)? See Colossians 1:9-10.

8. Hebrews 13:15 speaks of the fruit of our lips. How can we apply it to our thoughts?

9. Read Psalm 119: 9-11. What is a tangible way to fight the temptations of unruly thoughts?

Our enemy is called The Accuser. If your thoughts are accusing you, they may originate from him. The Holy Spirit does not harshly condemn, but brings us gently and kindly to repentance (Romans 2:4). Any thoughts that are shaming or blaming are definitely not of God. Any what-ifs or worries about the future are also not God's will for your mind. Take these thoughts "prisoner of war" and throw them in jail (2 Corinthians 10:5). Refuse to entertain them, but replace them with good thoughts. Recite Scripture or worship song lyrics filled with hope and God's love. Declare the promises of God, even out loud if you must!

Again, our enemy may not give up without a fight and this may be a very difficult battle at first. Remember to pray and ask God for help (Ephesians 6:18). Utilize the other weapons at your disposal as well. Remind yourself of Ephesians 6:16:

> *In all circumstances take up the shield of faith, with which you can extinguish all the flaming darts of the evil one. (ESV)*

Read about Jesus' ordeal of temptation in Matthew 4:1-11.

10. With what did Satan try to tempt Jesus?

11. Why would these things have been attractive to Jesus' humanity?

12. How and with what did Jesus respond?

13. What comfort do we receive from 1 Corinthians 10:13?

In her book, Becky Harling wrote a section entitled, "Commit to Saturating Your Mind with Scripture, To Zero Tolerance for Satan's messages."

> We are called to be holy, just as God is holy (1 Peter 1:15). How is this even possible? The psalmist gave us the answer: "How can a young man keep his way pure? By living according to your word." He went on, "I have hidden your word in my heart that I might not sin against you" (Psalm 119:9,11). Dear friend, if you don't saturate your mind with Scripture, it will automatically gravitate to your old script, because that's where it has become comfortable. It is the Holy Spirit's role to change you, but the more Scripture you memorize, the more you give Him to work with!
>
> The rewriting is an ongoing, lifelong process, not a one-time transaction. In many ways it is like peeling an onion. God peels back a layer, revealing a negative message written on our scripts and our sinful response to that message. We confess that sinful response, erase the lie, replace it with truth, and choose a godly attitude. God then peels back another layer and reveals another negative message and so on until our entire scripts are revised. This rewriting of our scripts takes a lifetime.

I have heard that memorizing Scripture "increases the Holy Spirit's vocabulary in your mind." As you have God's Word more readily available in the forefront of your thoughts, the Holy Spirit will use it to remind you of truth and encourage you.

Habitually Living Unselfishly

14. Read p. 108 in *Bitter Truth*. What is the ultimate remedy for bitterness?

15. Look up and ponder Galatians 5:14 and James 2:8. What are these commands called? Does this magnify their importance in your mind?

16. Read p. 109 in *Bitter Truth*, and review the chart on pp. 112-113. What would my life look like if I were entirely outward-focused?

17. Think about how this could be manifested in your life. Does it seem far-fetched? Why or why not?

18. Think of a young child you know. What do they mostly talk about? What are some of their needs or cravings? How do they demonstrate immaturity and selfishness?

19. Do we easily outgrow these desires as we become adults?

20. Read 1 Corinthians 13:11, 1 Corinthians 14:20, and Galatians 5:13. What is the common thread in these verses? How can you summarize these admonitions?

This verse directs us to forsake our selfish desires (the cravings of youth or immaturity), and to place our focus on pursuing righteousness, love, and other fruits of the Spirit. We move forward in this pursuit along with our like-minded brothers and sisters. We are focusing outwardly, thinking of encouraging others in the same race, all the while putting off or setting aside our own desires.

21. What are some practical ways we can do this within the body of believers? Review James 5, especially verses 9, 11, 13-15, and19-20.

Review the chart in *Bitter Truth*, pp. 61-62. This shows the contrast between selfish and unselfish reactions to a variety of scenarios: friendship, family, job, and church life.

22. In which of these situations do you struggle the most to be unselfish?

We must train ourselves in habits and immerse ourselves in practices that keep us going the direction we want to go. Sailing a very small degree off course is not a big deal if you're only going a mile across a lake, but if you're traveling across the ocean you'll end up on the wrong continent! Our journey will take a lifetime and is much more akin to a marathon than a sprint. We need to train our minds to think automatically of others, which will serve us well over the long haul.

A.W. Tozer said, "You will never be more than a common Christian until you give up your own interests and cease defending yourself."

I like his use of the term "defending yourself." We protect and cover ourselves when we withdraw into self-pity, selfishness, or fear. We must stop thinking of ourselves and being defensive in order to truly love others. I call this *Inward Thinking vs. Outward Living*.

In *Inward Thinking*, the focus is all on me. I am the center of my own little universe. I'm carefully judging how everyone else responds or reacts to me. I am busy deciding what they think of me, based on my close observations. I compare whether I'm sought out, liked, or given as much attention as others.

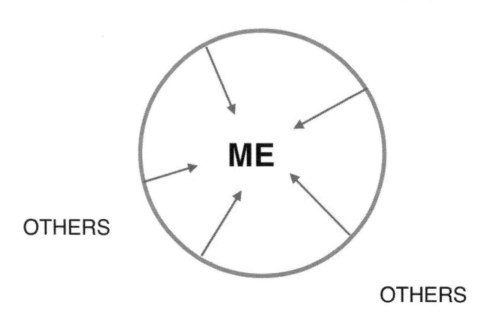

Inward Thinking

OTHERS

ME

OTHERS

OTHERS

This kind of thinking will inevitably lead to depression and anger as I observe that I'm *not* the center of attention and I'm *not* receiving as much consideration as I had hoped for. This is entirely selfish thinking and leads me down the path to envy, hurt, anger, and bitterness.

Outward Living means that I am placing my focus on those around me. I essentially forget about myself in my efforts to reach out to others. I am thinking about how to bless them, how to encourage them, how to make them feel important and liked. I speak words that will build them up and point them to Christ. I ask questions that show I'm interested in their lives and activities. I don't even notice who pays attention to me, because I'm so occupied with reaching out. I'm acting outwardly—offensively—so that I am not thinking about being defensive.

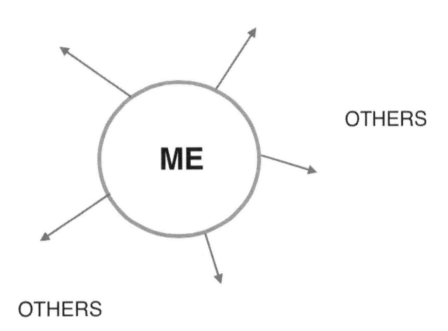

Outward Living

OTHERS

OTHERS

ME

OTHERS

This is how Jesus lived and interacted with others. He never once stopped in the middle of ministering or teaching to ask, "Who is taking care of *me*? Who asks about *my* needs?" He cared for others even while dragging a cross to His execution. He spoke tenderly to His mother and the thief on the cross next to Him while enduring unimaginable suffering. What an example of unselfish love!

23. Ephesians 6:18 tells us to be alert and do what?

Unselfish love takes constant practice, so that over time it becomes a habit.

Developing A Grateful Mindset

Yes, we know we're supposed to be thankful. But what if you don't see much to be thankful for in your life? What if it's hard for you to give thanks?

Good habits can be learned. How does one become a marathon runner? He or she doesn't just wake up one day and say, "I am now a marathon runner." We know that is ridiculous. It involves a decision and a goal. One day Bob wakes up and says, "I'm going to start training for the marathon that will be held in my city nine months from now." And from that day on, he follows a training regimen that moves him toward that goal. He runs faithfully and regularly, even in bad weather and when he doesn't feel like it. On the day of the race, Bob runs the marathon and becomes a marathon runner. But the process started many months before and involved making the right choices each day.

We can always find something to be thankful for, in every situation. I am reminded of a story of two neighbors who had their homes demolished in a tornado. The news reporter interviewed one woman, and she complained about how slow the authorities were in responding and how she hadn't had a hot meal in over 24 hours. Then they interviewed her neighbor. He said, "You can replace stuff, but you can't replace family!" and he was so thankful that they were all alive and safe. These people were in the *exact* same situation, yet one chose self-pity and the other chose gratitude.

So make the choice today that you are going to become a thankful person. With God's help, you are going to become someone who has an attitude of gratitude and is continually giving Him thanks. Let's make choosing gratitude such a habit that we can hardly remember what self-pity looks like! Following are some guidelines for your "training regimen" and steps to follow in this process.

Think About What You're Thinking About

We discussed the technique of metacognition earlier in this lesson and divided our thoughts into 3 categories: neutral, negative, and positive. First, decide that you are not going to tolerate negative thoughts of any kind once you become aware of them. Stomp out all ANTS!

I've said this before, but it bears repeating because it is so important: **Beware self-pitying thoughts**. Self-pity is especially dangerous because we do it to comfort ourselves. It feels good! But it leads to other negative thoughts, especially envy, and down a slippery slope from there. Nothing good ever comes from self-pity. Fight any thoughts such as these, and replace them with thanksgiving. They are at the opposite ends of a spectrum: you can either be one or the other, but *never both*.

Self-Pity   Thanksgiving

2 Corinthians 10:5 tells us to take captive all such negative thoughts and make them obedient to Christ. I remember when I was first beginning this process, I would reject the negative thought and replace it with something positive. But not five minutes later, I would find my mind returning to the same old loop of self-pity, or envy, or anger. I would have to do it again and again and again! The grooves in my brain (or maybe the enemy) wanted to take me down into the same old pit, and it was a real fight to consistently change the direction of my thoughts.

Watch Your Words

Sometimes we're not aware of our negative thoughts until we say something and think, *"Where did that come from?"* We know that the words we speak are an overflow of what's in our hearts and minds (Luke 6:45), so words of criticism or complaining can be a wake-up call. It is evidence that our minds are not flowing in a Spirit-led or transformed direction.

24. What three things are listed in Ephesians 5:4 as opposed to giving thanks? Why should we not engage in them?

25. Philippians 2:14-15 tells us to do everything without what? How is this activity the opposite of gratitude?

Jon Bloom speaks of gratitude versus grumbling:

> *Grumbling is a gauge of the human soul. It gauges our gaze on grace. It tells us we're not seeing grace. Grumbling is a symptom of a near-sighted or myopic soul. Gratitude is a symptom of a healthy, expansive soul. Gratitude is the accent of the language of heaven, because there everything is undeserved grace. Grumbling is the accent of hell's language, because it's how a creature's pride responds to the Creator's decision to do or to allow something that the creature does not desire. Grumbling scorns God because it elevates our desires and judgments above His. Philippians 2:14-15 do everything without grumbling and complaining.... Those who have been forgiven so much (Luke 7:47) and promised so much (2 Peter 1:4), should speak words that are always salted with gratitude (Ephesians 5:20). Gratitude requires seeing grace. ~ from Don't Follow Your Heart*

Develop Holy Habits

It's not enough to fight our negative thoughts alone. We must *replace them* with something good. After all, nature abhors a vacuum, right? So with what specifically should we fill our minds?

In the last lesson, we discussed truth versus lies and some specific things the Bible tells us to think on (review Lesson 9, question #17).

Just as lies and negative thoughts can become habits, we must consciously seek to establish holy habits in our lives. What do I mean by that? Mimi Wilson and Shelly Volkhardt have written the book *Holy Habits*. These godly ladies were retreat speakers at our church, and I have sat under their teaching several times. One habit Shelly mentioned was while she is driving, she would pick out specific landmarks that reminded her of someone or something. Then she would regularly pray for that need or person whenever she saw that landmark. It could be a fence, a building, or even a stoplight. The other day I drove by the neighborhood where a friend lives and was prompted to pray for some needs in her family. A local bank may remind you of someone's financial need, or a street sign similar to someone's name may provoke you to pray for them. Some ladies pray for their children while they are folding their laundry and pray for their husbands while changing the bed linens. Whatever prompts you to pray faithfully for others is a good habit to establish.

I describe another habit for giving thanks on pp.123-124 of *Bitter Truth*. Read it and think of some ways you could incorporate this habit into your daily routine. Maybe you could regularly practice it with your children in the car or around the dinner table.

And lastly, develop the holy habit of memorizing God's Word. This practice was a significant factor that promoted the healing and transformation of my thoughts. For years, I was a carpooling mom and spent hours each day in the car. This was part of the problem: since I didn't need to think about driving the same route each day, my thoughts were able to wander. And guess where they routinely went? I meditated on the people who had wronged me and how unfair it all was. I pondered my lonely childhood and re-lived the years of pain and rejection. I compared my husband to others, which prompted dissatisfaction and anger. I often worked myself up into a rage or dissolved into tears. And this just from driving to school and back!

How can you memorize Scripture if you haven't done it before? Photocopy some verses from your Bible and carry them around constantly. It helps to laminate them, if you can. Read them through every time you have a spare minute. After a few times, try saying them back without looking. Choose verses that speak to particular struggles you have, like fear, worry, or anger. Or some great chapters to start with are Romans 8, Colossians 3, Ephesians 1, Psalm 103, and Psalm 23. I did this while driving carpool. At every red light, I picked up my sheet and read the verses out loud. Then while driving, I'd try to recite them back.

Like I said, this habit was life-changing for me. It helped me control my thoughts and increased the Holy Spirit's vocabulary in my brain.

Develop holy habits of regularly giving thanks, praying for others, and filling your mind with God's Word. They will transform the way you think!

Look For the Good

26. Read Jeremiah 17:5-8.

Cursed is the one who_____.

He/she will be like a _____ and *will not see*

_____.

In contrast, (verse 7) blessed is the one who _____.

How is he/she described in verse 8?

Gratitude consists in a watchful, minute attention to the particulars of our state, and to the multitude of God's gifts, taken one by one...
When I notice and remember what God has done, I will see the pattern of God's work in my life. I decided that I would focus on what is known as "common grace." Common grace is what we experience in the normal things of life. When I chose to dwell on the normal, daily things that God provided for my family and me, I began also to appreciate His generous hand in spiritual areas of my life. ~ from Holy Habits

Here's a small example of this. I was looking at my calendar for next week and planning my schedule. We will have a church staff meeting in a few days. My pastor/boss/friend Doug was away ministering last weekend. I am looking forward to seeing him and asking all about his weekend. I will tell him we prayed for him and hope to hear a favorable report.

If you've read my book, you know the story of Doug and me and our difficult relationship. Isn't this remarkable? In the past, I would have dreaded seeing him and not been concerned about his ministry. I would have only been thinking of myself. What a work God has done in me and in him! Praise God, from whom all blessings flow. Thank you Lord, *again*, for what you did there!

But it would have been easy to just gloss over the meeting notification and think, "Oh yeah, Doug will be back." Instead, I'm *looking for* the good. I'm looking for things to thank God for. The healing of our relationship is something I will be thankful for, for years to come.

We will grow in the habit of cultivating gratitude through the exercise of the constant practice of looking for grace.

David Powlinson wrote "The Anti-Psalm 23 of the Unbeliever" which is the polar opposite of Psalm 23. It describes perfectly the thoughts of the person in Jeremiah 17:5-6:

> *I'm on my own. No one looks out for me or protects me.*
> *I experience a continual sense of need. Nothing's quite right.*
> *I'm always restless. I'm easily frustrated and often disappointed.*
> *It's a jungle—I feel overwhelmed. It's a desert—I'm thirsty.*
> *My soul feels broken, twisted, and stuck. I can't fix myself.*
> *I stumble down some dark paths.*
> *Still, I insist: I want to do what I want, when I want, how I want.*
> *But life's confusing. Why don't things ever really work out?*
> *I'm haunted by emptiness and futility—shadows of death.*
> *I fear the big hurt and final loss.*
> *Death is waiting for me at the end of every road, but I'd rather not think about that.*
> *I spend my life protecting myself. Bad things can happen.*
> *I find no lasting comfort. I'm alone... facing everything that could hurt me.*
> *Are my friends really friends? Other people use me for their own ends.*
> *I can't really trust anyone. No one has my back.*
> *No one is really for me—except me.*
> *And I'm so much all about ME, sometimes it's sickening.*
> *I belong to no one except myself. My cup is never quite full enough.*
> *I'm left empty. Disappointment follows me all the days of my life.*
> *Will I just be obliterated into nothingness?*
> *Will I be alone forever, homeless, free-falling into void?*
> *Sartre said, "Hell is other people."*
> *I have to add, "Hell is also myself." It's a living death, and then I die.*

Now, for a refreshing contrast, read slowly and carefully through Psalm 23. Rejoice in the goodness and promises of our loving Shepherd who guides us, invites us to rest, and is pursuing us with His goodness, love, and mercy.

Keep Your Eyes Up

At the Last Supper, shortly before Jesus' death, the Bible says:

And he took bread, and when he <u>had given thanks,</u> he broke it and gave it to them, saying, "This is my body, which is given for you. Do this in remembrance of me." (Luke 22:19)

Bloom says:

> *Jesus' thanks was not based on His present circumstances. He was about to endure the worst possible horror. He felt thankful to the Father for the grace and glory that was coming because of the cross, and this gave Him joy. That's where God wants your eyes: on the future joy He has promised you.*

> *For the joy set before him he endured the cross, scorning its shame, and sat down at the right hand of the throne of God. (Hebrews 12:2 NIV)*

Could this be said of you?

"For the joy set before him/her, (*Your name here*) endured (*fill in the blank*) and gave thanks."

27. What is the command in Colossians 3:1-2?

28. Read John 14:1-4. What is Jesus promising in these verses?

29. Why did He say this to His disciples? (v. 1)

30. How can this stimulate hope and cultivate gratitude?

Some of my favorite worship songs are on this topic. Here's a list of a few that speak of the future and the hope we have:

When the Stars Burn Down by Travis Cottrell
Soon by Hillsong United
Even So Come by Kristian Stanfill
Glorious Day by Casting Crowns
Revelation Song by Phillips, Craig and Dean
Home by Chris Tomlin

Listen and sing and fill your minds with these rich lyrics!

Make A Memorial

In the Old Testament, the Israelites built monuments to commemorate a time when they met with God or the actions of God on their behalf. One such altar was at the Jordan River. God parted the waters so they could enter the Promised Land on dry ground (Joshua 4:20-22). The stones were a reminder to future generations of the miraculous action God performed there.

Jesus instructed the disciples to remember Him by observing the Lord's Supper regularly. We still do that today in many churches. Why? We need to be reminded often of Jesus' love and sacrifice for us on the cross. It seems we are forgetful people and prone to forget God's goodness.

To give thanks well, we must remember well what God has done for us and for others. We must share these stories often. Giving testimony of answered prayer or miraculous provision in our lives boosts our faith and provokes gratitude.

> When "What-Ifs" come into our lives, we must ask ourselves if we're going to judge God by the circumstances we don't understand or judge the circumstances in light of the character of God… We survive the packages of pain God allows in our lives by remembering who God is and what He has done in the past." ~ Linda Dillow, from Calm My Anxious Heart

We need tools or symbols to help us remember. I'm not suggesting you go stack up stones in your front yard, but do something tangible to help you remember God's faithfulness in your life. It could be as simple as journaling your prayers and struggles.

I was prompted to thanksgiving just recently while reading an old journal. I came across a prayer I had written while very frustrated in a relationship. I asked the Lord to help me react well, no matter what. I rejoiced as I thought of that relationship today. God prevented me from saying something I would regret, and the relationship is better than ever! However, I had *completely forgotten* about that situation until I read the journal.

Remember the story of Joseph? Read Genesis 41:51-52.

31. What do Manasseh and Ephraim mean?

32. Why would Joseph have given them these names?

Joseph made a choice to intentionally forget all the hardships he had been through. He was not going to dwell on them or engage in any self-pity. He demonstrated this by naming his firstborn son Manasseh: "making to forget." By this action, he was creating a permanent memorial; it was his intention *not to* remember the wrongs done to him or the injustices he survived. It was also a testimony to his brothers of his promise to forgive and forget the past.

When his second son was born, he again bestowed a meaningful name: Ephraim, which means "making fruitful." He was thanking God and giving testimony to His blessings in Joseph's life. He said: "For God has made me fruitful in the land of my affliction."

This is powerful evidence of transformed thinking on Joseph's part. Every time he called his sons over to him, he would remember what their names meant and that he had chosen to forget the painful past and give thanks to God. In modern day terms, we could picture a woman who had been freed and forgiven of bitterness naming her daughters "Hope" and "Joy." What a wonderful, constant reminder this would be!

33. What kind of tangible memorial can you make to help remember what God has done in your life?

Persevere and Be Patient

Lastly, read *Bitter Truth* p. 124. I talk about the process of being transformed in a necessarily brief narrative, but there were many days of discouragement, failure, and tears. I sent up many frustrated and angry prayers to God during this process.

The important thing is to keep moving in the same direction. Keep trusting that God is working and will transform you. Keep praying, keep asking, and keep believing. And look for the good work that He's promised He will do in you! (Philippians 1:6)

Jesus replied, "What is impossible with man is possible with God." (Luke 18:27)

Application:

A. Identify some habits in your thinking that you would like to change.
B. Think about some new, holy habits you would like to establish.
C. Develop a plan for creating new habits in the next month.

It is always possible to be thankful for what is given rather than resentful over what is withheld. One attitude or the other becomes a way of life. ~ Elisabeth Elliot

Made in the USA
Middletown, DE
24 February 2022

61704917R00068